I Get To Prepare My Heart

I Get To Prepare My Heart

A CHRISTMAS DEVOTIONAL

~

Cindy L Pentecost

ISBN-13: 9781977774385
ISBN-10: 1977774385

Contents

Advent

~

THIS WORD COMES FROM A Latin word meaning "coming". A season of preparation.

Every Christmas season, a few days after Thanksgiving I join a friend or two and prepare my heart to be ready to enjoy each moment of the days leading up to Christmas. Since "Christ" is the center of Christmas, I find a 31-day devotional that will turn my heart and mind towards His thoughts.

So why did I write this book? Simply, because The Lord asked me to. He wants each of you to know what he tells me every day. HE LOVES US! He thinks about us...ALL the time, and oh the precious moments He longs to share with us.

I don't want us to miss a thing He has for us but with the season comes.... drumroll please...BUSYNESS! BUSYNESS! BUSYNESS!

The enemy definitely does not want me or you to be centered in the season of peace, joy, love, simplicity, giving, receiving, sacrifice, serving and rest.

I discovered several years ago, I had a deliberate choice to be front and center with my savior during this most sacred season.

For so many of us this is our "favorite time of year," and yet, it is also one where the frenzied hustle and bustle can take all the joy right out of us.

We feel the "I have to" version of ourselves often casting a shadow of dread over the glorious days of this season.

When I finished the "I Get To" Conference in 2016, I began praying what was His will for the next thing for me...and what I heard this past year was, "An Advent book leading with 'I Get To' celebrate all that Christmas is.

God has so gently reminded me about how my mother, a single mom of six girls, every year right after Thanksgiving began working a second job at Sears. And I reflected how exhausted she must have already been but she never once complained. As children, we definitely had our chores to do and helping out around the house. Yet she made time to always have the tree up, decorations around the house, singing carols to nursing homes, baking special holidays favorites, shopping, worship and children's programs we were involved in.

She kept Christ the main part of Christmas, yet we definitely believed in Santa and all that is good about a man with those characteristics. I'm sure I recall a few reminders too, if I wasn't good I'd get nothing for Christmas. She kept the wonder of Christmas so well I believed in Santa until 6th grade.

Why bring all this into the conversation? My mother was amazing but by no means did she do it right 100% of the time. I'm sure she felt guilt from being gone in the morning at 7:00 until nearly 11:00 every night during those holiday times. She did not work Sundays and we made the most of that family time together.

We as women are just too hard on ourselves. We expect from ourselves what no one else does and what we would never expect from others.

And I know as Jesus looks down on each of us, He longs to help us know, we are loved and accepted. He is proud to call us his children. We are more than enough regardless of what we do get done or leave for another day.

I'm praying that daily you'll pick up this little book and enjoy a few moments to pause and reflect and get a glimpse of our amazing Savior. To get a fresh view of yourself and your days through His eyes.

At the end of each day there is a place to write down at least three things that you are grateful for. There is also a place to journal what you "Get to do."

I love you, and I'm so honored to be reading these pages right alongside you.

May His presence be so near to you and give you a joy-filled Christmas.

Cindy

"May the God of hope fill you with all Joy and Peace as you trust in Him, so that you may overflow." Romans 15:13

Take Away the Clutter

ONE OF THE FIRST THINGS I do to prepare my home for decorating is declutter the shelves. Put away things that are not Christmas, making room for the things that are. Dust off the shelves and prepare my house to be transformed into "all things Christmas."

I love pulling out the decorations and putting little Christmas touches everywhere. But it can also be exhausting. Pushing and pulling things out of storage, putting away all those extra things I don't want on the shelves. Exchanging non-seasonal pillows for the beautiful Christmas ones. You can all identify in some degree.

I love having friends and family enter our home and know through messages in the decorations that in our home, Christ is the center and we love to celebrate His coming. If I left things all cluttered the message might be confusing if not at least hard to follow. It is not so much about how much one has, but rather to use what you do have to display special sights, sounds and smells of Christmas, making our homes feel peaceful. One where any who come in can rest and enjoy a piece of Christmas.

Now to be honest, especially in the early days of marriage, I could get rather frustrated as I pridefully thought "I have to" do all this by myself. Oh, it was always me pushing to do these things, with each season came new decorations going up and down. No one was making me do it, but it is part of my DNA. I love the days I have help from friends, and Mark is a wonderful help too, offering to restack boxes, pull things down from shelves. Take the ladder in and out.

These days I do not take for granted the joy I get from decorating our home. You see, I don't have to decorate at all; I Get To take time clearing away the clutter to make room for the beauty awaiting to enter the rooms.

It is like this with my time alone with God, too. As I prepare my heart each morning, "I Get To" sit and be still. "I Get To" lift up my family and friends in prayer. "I Get To" hear, through His word the wisdom to live according to His plan, one day at a time. It is very much a time spent with a very real, loving, caring savior and friend.

If a friend were coming for tea, I would light a candle, have a special place where the two of us could talk. I'd clear any distractions. I would put my phone aside so it wouldn't distract the special time we set aside together. I would want her to know, she has my full attention. I want to hear her; the rest of the world can wait. When I finish my time with my friends; I feel rested.

So, it is with Jesus. He is my friend. Did you know he calls us his friend?

"I no longer call you servants, because a servant does not know his master's business. I have called you friends, for everything that I have learned from my Father I have made known unto you." John 15:15

My time with friends is something I treasure.

"A sweet friendship refreshes the soul" Proverbs 27:9

Dear Jesus,

Thank you that you call me, (insert your name) your friend. That you desire for me to spend time with you so you can tell me everything you have learned from your Father. Today, help me be willing to set everything else aside and just listen. Just be with you. Please help me understand how my friendship with you can and will refresh my soul. Lord, I do not have to spend time with you, but just like "I Get To" prepare my home for the Christmas season, give me a deep desire and the realization that "I Get To" spend time with you.

Father, please show me if there is some clutter in my life distracting me from your best plan. Thank you for what Christmas means. Help me grasp it more. Help me to think about you all day long. Help me to worship you by doing all "I Get To" do with a grateful heart and to do all I do as unto you.

I love you Jesus. Thank you for coming to prepare my heart to fully receive you in all things big and small today. I thank you for the preparation you are doing in my heart to be transformed into your image.

In Jesus' precious name,

AMEN

Today I am grateful for: _____   _____

_____

Today I Get To..._____

_____

_____

_____

_____

_____

_____

_____

_____

_____

_____

_____

_____

_____

_____

_____

_____

_____

The Smells of Christmas

THE SMELLS OF CHRISTMAS ARE something I love to place all around our home.

I love how certain scents can immediately transport us into different seasons, holidays, and stir up special childhood memories.

Beginning when I was a child and until our children were almost grown we would put up a real tree. Some years we did the outing to the Christmas tree farm. Those memories of riding the sleigh wagons through the snow with the sting of cold hitting our faces all the while singing carols. Choosing just the right tree, drinking hot cocoa, and oh, the smell of that freshly cut tree. All wonderful memories. Whether we went to a nearby tree lot or did the grand adventure, getting the tree up always brought that fresh scent of pine into our home.

I always associate the smell of pine with the Christmas season. I place pine and evergreen candles around the house. It immediately smells like Christmas.

When I'm spending my quiet time with the Lord, candlelight always seems to offer a sense of intimacy. Often, my time with Jesus is in the middle of the night. I have often thought about what it was like for Jesus as he woke early and spent time with His Father. I am also moved to consider if Jesus, being who he is, felt it such a priority to spend time alone with His Father, how much more does this time I invest help me become who He created me to be.

"Very early in the morning, while it was still dark, Jesus got up, left the house and went off *to a solitary place, where he prayed." Mark 1:35*

God's word tells us we are made in his image (Genesis 1:27).

I love and treasure memories. I love how quickly one of the five senses can transport us into a different time and place. As this message was being whispered to my heart that since I am made in His image, these things must be precious to Him as well. I asked the Lord, what would be a memory stirred in Him by a specific scent. This is the image He brought to my mind.

"Then Mary took about a pint of pure nard, an expensive perfume; she poured it out on Jesus feet and wiped his feet with her hair. And the house was filled with the fragrance of the perfume." John 12:3

What a wonderful memory of being loved and adored. We all long to feel loved and even adored. Often, we go to great lengths looking for this in so many wrong places. Much of what we do can be for this very approval and love. When we look to man to give us this deep love and devotion we often have unmet expectations for it is God alone that can do this filling up of our soul's longings.

"Human approval is a dangerous trap, but trusting in the Lord means safety." Proverbs 29:25

I love these scents that stir memories of days where love and laughter filled the air. These are gifts that continue on long after the actual event has passed by.

I wonder what you may be doing today that if you took time to honestly evaluate it, you might be hoping to fill a longing that has gone unmet for many years.

The Christmas season with all the scents and beauty, cannot begin to match the matchless love and beauty that the Christ child offers to each of us.

He is here with us every moment of every day. He is waiting for us to turn to Him and allow our hearts to pour out a sacrifice of praise that will be much like Mary who poured out the expensive perfume.

Jesus knows what it costs you to set aside all you have to do and entrust he will replenish the time you "Get To" spend with him in glorious and mysterious ways.

You "Get To" choose to light a candle, you "Get To" take a moment to sit with Jesus. You "Get To" let Him be the one who can fill any void you have.

And in choosing to do this you "Get To" be a light to those in your world.

Dear Jesus,

Thank you for the gift of scents that stir up precious memories I hold so close in my heart. Lord, today help me be a fragrant offering in all I do and say. And may all I do be an act of worship, knowing a grateful heart precedes the peace you promise to give. As I go about my day, please remind me that I Get To celebrate you; I Get To be the gift someone needs today. I Get To share The Greatest Gift ever given—YOU!

In Jesus' name,

Amen

Today I am grateful for:_____   _____

_____

Today I Get To.... _____

_____

_____

_____

_____

_____

_____

_____

_____

_____

Sounds of Christmas

IT IS TRULY AMAZING HOW each year the signs and sounds of Christmas are seen and heard earlier and earlier. We barely have time to celebrate Thanksgiving before the 'ALL-NIGHT SHOPPING" cries are going out. The papers are so filled with ads and early bird deals we can fall into the temptation to forget we are spending the day "giving thanks".

I begin to shift all my music to the songs of Christmas right after Thanksgiving. I love the old Bing Crosby and Karen Carpenter favorites (just to name a few), as well as the newer songs. All types of Christmas music is in full swing.

As I begin doing the decorating, baking, even shopping, I love hearing the Christmas music. It somehow helps me get more enthusiastic about whatever task I'm doing for that day.

Since our move to Florida, music is even more important as the "natural" signs of the season aren't anywhere to be found. There is no chill in the air and no snow on the ground. The trees are not freshly cut and often no longer have that scent of fresh pine. That being said, the sounds, smells, decorations and other tell-tale signs that Christmas is truly around the corner are very helpful.

Music is an amazing phenomenon that can trigger all sorts of emotions. For me, when I hear the old favorites I get in the mood to get after the decorating, the baking, the shopping, the wrapping, and well, you get the idea.

One of the greatest aha moments I had in my walk with the Lord came shortly after the move to Florida and during the first Christmas season here. I realized my heart was more tied to the traditional sights and sounds of Christmas than the strings that tied my heart to the Lord.

You see, if one of my children or my husband is having a birthday, no one needs to give me "the signs" that it is their birthday season. I know when it is, I am preparing to celebrate and regardless of what songs or other seasonal clues are obvious, they are not necessary. I am so tied to their hearts that nothing could distract me from celebrating them.

I was struck by just how much Christmas didn't feel or seem like Christmas without the snow and cold that I was so accustomed to. It was even easy to ignore that Christmas was coming. I was very moved to realize that much of what I had made Christmas about was not the Christ Child. If you ask me what the reason for the season is I would undoubtedly share the birth of Jesus Christ.

Please don't misunderstand me, I loved growing up in Michigan. All the memories are a deep part of who I am. I even miss a white Christmas and a fresh snow fall. I asked God to show me how to allow the true spirit of Christmas, the Holy Spirit, to fill me with a heightened awareness of things that would trigger deeper longings to be more engaged and prepared to celebrate Jesus.

We joke in our home that we have birthday seasons. Generally, the month of your birthday is your birthday season. Well I can think of no one who deserve a Birthday Month more than Jesus, the one who created each of us.

It is important to say, I never felt condemned as I began realizing what had slowly happened over the years. I just felt a hug from God, gently telling me that He loves spending time with me. And I know He longs to have you know this very same thing.

"The Lord your God is in your midst, a mighty one who will save; He will rejoice over you with gladness; he will quiet you by His love; He will exult over you with loud signing." Zephaniah 3:17

As you begin preparing for Christmas by listening to the songs you love, be sure to mix in some songs that will direct your heart and mind to Jesus. Let truth fill you up as you sing along to the lyrics. Fill your home with songs of true deliverance and songs that offer up worship and praise to Him for this incredible gift He has given to us.

"Sing joyfully, to the Lord, you righteous. It is fitting for the upright to praise Him." Psalm 33:1

Dear Jesus,

Thank you for your love and passion for me every day. Please examine my heart and show me any place where I have allowed tradition to crowd out the simplicity of an honest longing and searching for ways to worship and celebrate all you have done for me. Please show me special unique ways for you and me to connect on a deeper level. I long for my home to be filled with praises going up to you and for all to know You are the reason I love and celebrate Christmas.

In Jesus' name,

Amen

Today I am grateful for: _____   _____

_____

Today I Get To: _____

_____

_____

_____

_____

_____

_____

_____

_____

The Tree

THERE IS JUST SOMETHING SPECIAL about putting the Christmas tree up. The traditions your family has created together. The lights, whether multi-color or all white, always make the room feel so warm. The music playing and the sweet voices singing along. Maybe your family strings popcorn or makes those red and green construction paper chains. Then there are the memories attached to the special ornaments, the "Oh mom, do you remember this one?" and the giggles as we look at how little and young we all looked as they are gently lifted out of the boxes. Each family treasuring this capsulated time steeped in tradition.

There is something really special about watching adult children carry these traditions into their home, mixing two families' treasured traditions and beginning new and magical Christmas memories. But there is also that strange feeling when you find yourself decorating without the kids. It can seem somewhat hollow if you're not careful to be sure and remember you Get To...decorate your home and create new memories with your new normal. You Get To watch and be a special part of your adult children's lives.

The first few years of doing the decorating without the kids, I was intentional to find new ways to decorate my home. I Get To put the music on, light the candles and enjoy time with special friends to usher out what could have otherwise been the awkward silence and obvious absence of the days gone by.

The evergreen tree holds a hidden message that can remind us to embrace life. These special moments and choosing to live life to the fullest are things to be treasured. We Get To give thanks that we have our faith, dear friends, and the love of family. We Get To serve others and be the joy that some really need at this time of year. We Get To open these gifts daily that the Lord provides and be a voice of Hope and Love.

It is a gift to treasure life; sadly, many leave this treasure unopened and miss the very purpose of life. Some have had some hard things happened to them or they feel they've made so many bad choices that they don't deserve to be happy. Satan would like nothing more than to rob them of the "joy-filled, freedom in Christ" life that Jesus longs to give them. It is why He came.

"The thief comes to kill steal and destroy. But Jesus said this: "I come that they may have life and may have it abundantly." John 10:10

You see, just as an evergreen tree never loses it color, regardless of the environment, it is as its name implies… always green.

And the very reason Jesus came as a baby, born in a lowly manger was for you and me to have a life that never ends. Regardless of where we find ourselves today, where we have been or what we have done: Eternal life with Jesus can be our reality. It is not dependent on what you do, but on what Jesus already did.

"For this is how God loved the world: He gave His one and only son, so that everyone who believes in Him will not perish but have eternal life." John 3:16

If you have never received Jesus as your personal Lord and Savior, it is done by a simple prayer. Just begin by talking to Jesus and ask Him to forgive you of anything you've done in your past. Tell Him that you are sorry and want to receive Him as your Lord and Savior, and thank Him for all He has done for you. Close that simple prayer in the name of Jesus, and you will be saved.

If you did say that prayer, this Christmas will hold new joy and wonder for you than you have ever experienced before.

As with a real tree, it needs water and sunlight if it is to grow. So it is with us and our relationship with Jesus. Spend this time going through this devotional, and simply pray for God to show you things that you would otherwise not see or know. Ask Him to help you recognize the blessings that He places in your life and for Him to grow a heart of gratitude in you.

Just as the evergreen tree does not have to do something to remain green, your salvation is not based on what you can do. This relationship is watered by spending time with Jesus and will grow by the workings of Him in your life.

"Being confident of this, that He who began a good work in you will carry it on to completion until the day of Christ Jesus.". Philippians 1:6

Dear Precious Lord and Savior,

Thank you for all you have done to make it possible for you and me to have a close relationship. I am humbled and grateful to be called your child. Help me to know just how to receive this love and grow our relationship. Protect my heart and mind to remember that this is not something I earned. But also rise up in me a hunger for your Word and a longing to spend time with you. Bring other believers into my life so I can grow and have support as I Get To do life with you every day by my side.

I love you and I thank you for the gift of my salvation. Help me share my story with someone today that needs this same hope.

In Jesus' name,

Amen

Today I am grateful for: _____   _____

_____

Today I Get To: _____

_____

_____

_____

A Different Kind of Christmas

GOD HAS A TENDER MESSAGE for us this morning. He knows that many find themselves in a very different place. They are His children, He loves them, and they love Him in return. But the reality for them is that they would rather skip the celebrations this year. Because of deep losses, they are often subject to a slumbering soul. The grief has placed scales on their eyes to change the way they view their world. They have erected bars around their heart for fear of the weight of grief they carry to be too heavy. To just continue on this Christmas like previous years is just not possible; nor should it be.

Jesus wants to whisper some things to your sad and weary heart.

He sees you. He knows just the day to day living has often found you in those desert places, parched and thirsty yet unable to get to the well. You have learned to thank Him for the hard and difficult journey and have seen His peace blossom in the most desolate places. You are more aware than ever of your dependence on Him to just keep going, one day at a time.

But this holiday shines a light on the hollow of your heart. While others speak of decorating and holiday shopping you can barely breath. You just want to sit with the one you lost one more day.

Jesus wants to remind you that you will one day sit with them again, but in the gap, He sits ready to listen to every cry. He will infuse His peace into your innermost being. The key to finding peace in this Christmas season is to quietly sit in the Light of His presence and wait on Him. You will sense Peace growing within you.

"Jesus is your refuge and strength, a very present help in this time of trouble." Psalm 46:1

Today is a perfect day to persevere in complete dependence on Jesus. If you had to drag yourself out of bed, know this: ALL days are perfect days to depend on Him to carry you through in childlike faith.

"God will make a way where there seems to be no way." Isaiah 43:16

The only way to adequately fill the cavern of loneliness and longing for what is no more is the awareness of God's abiding Presence. You can go to Him with your complete human honesty. You can tell Him anything you're feeling, and He alone can fill the hole that is your current day reality. He will sit and listen to you.

"O Lord, You have searched me and know me. You know when I sit and when I rise; you perceive my thoughts from afar. You discern my going out and my lying down; You are familiar with all of my ways. Before a word is on my tongue You know it completely, O Lord." Psalm 139:1-4

This next "I Get To" is hard because it is definitely a choice that is based on faith, not feelings. But we Get To engage this Christmas to show that when we are weak; He is strong. We Get To serve others when we don't feel like it because Jesus chose to die for us even when He didn't "feel like it."

Everyone grieves loss differently. I would never suggest I know what you are going through, even if I have been through something similar, because each situation is unique in and of itself.

What is a common thread? There is but One Christ:

"But we know that there is only one God, the Father, who created everything, and we live for Him. And there is only one Lord, Jesus Christ, through whom all things came and through Him we live." 1 Corinthians 8:6

When we go through extremely painful journeys in this life and when we choose to go through these valleys with Jesus by our side; I am always amazed to see how Christ's Love and Light shine though these faithful sons and daughters of God. These heroes of the faith are like the star that shone the night Jesus was born and lead the shepherds and wise men to where He lay.

As these who have lost so much find the strength to still rise, rejoice and be grateful for all He has done for them, they carry His light to a world that desperately needs Jesus.

Dear Jesus,

You are the King of Kings and the Lord of Lords, but you are also my Shepard, Companion and Friend. You are the one who never lets go of my hand. Thank you for being with me every day, especially on the days where I feel so low. I praise you for knowing everything about me. I thank you that you are my refuge and strength. Remind me each day of your faithfulness. Give me the desire to come into your presence and allow your Peace to engulf my weary soul. Help me reflect your glory and allow all of this is to transform me into your likeness so the world will see You through me.

Bind up my wounds and be in me all I lack today. Turn all my tears into prayers and do miracles through each one.

In Jesus' powerful name,

Amen

Today I am grateful for: _____   _____

_____

Today I Get To: _____

_____

_____

_____

_____

_____

_____

_____

_____

DECEMBER 6

The Perfect Gift

~

It may seem a little early to dive right into the gifts, but let's be honest, not getting our shopping done until the last minute adds stress. It's so hard to hear others talking about being completely done or better yet those who have been done shopping for months. REALLY! As if we aren't already hard enough on ourselves. When my children were at home I confess I was done with my shopping much earlier than I am these days. Somehow having so much to juggle and budget for made me more disciplined to getting those things done. It also seemed easier to get out of each family member what was on their wish list. These days I Get To be much more creative so I can find the perfect gifts.

I like choosing just the right gifts for each person I buy for. I love the look on their faces when I know they are going to love what I chose for them.

Another little tip: I ask God to direct my steps to find just the right gift that will bless that person. It's amazing, some of the ideas He has planted in my heart.

We aren't the originators of wanting to get the perfect gift for our family.

Listen to what God's Word says about His giving us; his beloved children the best gift.

"Even before He made the world, God loved us and chose us in Christ to be holy and without fault in His eyes. God decided in advance to adopt us

into His own family by bringing us to Himself through Jesus Christ. This is what He wanted to do, and it gave Him great pleasure. So, we praise God for the glorious grace He poured out on us who belong to His Dear Son. He is so rich in kindness and grace that He purchased our freedom with the blood of His son and forgave our sins. He has showered His kindness on us, along with all wisdom and understanding." Ephesians 1:4-8

We Get To be moved by this, We Get To allow this to change our preconceived beliefs about God. Regardless of what you might have been taught in your life, this Word is powerful.

I love my family, but I did not love them before they were even made. I loved the idea of them, but not them. I am also moved to see that when He looks at me He finds no fault. REALLY? It goes on to say that God wanted us to be His sons and daughters. He took pleasure in doing whatever that would take.

Consider this: He knew what it was going to take, and yet it still says it is what He wanted to do and it gave Him great pleasure. These are some of those mysteries that we simply won't fully comprehend until we see Him face to face.

The next thing we get to consider is this: When given the chance to be kind, do we shower kindness on people? Well since we are made in His image, we Get To shower kindness on others. What a gift that could be to so many who just need a little kindness, let alone to stand under a showering of it.

Let's consider something else in this scripture: The gifts given weren't bought but they were very costly. The sacrifice was priceless.

So, let's ask ourselves what is something we can give that does not cost us materially, but would require a different type of sacrificial giving.

We Get To consider what the needs are around us and how God has wired us to be someone who can meet these needs.

For example: Because I was raised by a single mom, I always asked God to place a single mom in my path. Then our family would bless her according to the need in loving memory and tribute to my mom's life. That is just one example of something that God uses to tug my heart into action.

Since you are reading this Advent devotional, I believe you desire to make room in your heart, mind and life for Jesus to be greater in you. I believe you have a desire for your life to bring Him glory. If you are married, get with your family and put some ideas of giving back though serving or helping someone in need. It can be really fun to get everyone involved. If you're single, get with a friend and go change at least one life together. It doesn't have to be some great life altering thing, although if that's how God leads you by all means go for it. But just getting someone's coffee or helping carry groceries out for an elderly person can be just what they needed to encourage them and help them feel the love of Jesus.

Dear Lord,

Thank you for choosing me before you even made the world. Thank you for loving me and finding no fault in me. Help me to see myself through your eyes. Thank you for adopting me as your own and for showering me with kindness. Help me know what you desire me to do to help someone else who is in a place of needing encouragement and love. Whether through an act of kindness or some tangible way of serving, direct my path. Give me a burning desire to shower kindness upon others. Open my eyes to see the ways I can richly bless those you place in my path this Christmas season.

In Jesus' name,

Amen

Today I am grateful for: _____   _____

_____

Today I Get To: _____

_____

_____

_____

In the Stillness of the Night

To be alone, in the stillness of the night
I dance with Jesus and look into his eyes
I get very still and shut out all the noise
So that I can hear His voice
My Savior is speaking
I recognize His voice
It's different than the rest
It's soft and gentle
There is wonder in His words
He knows I'm there to celebrate His coming
He is content to just sit with me and be still
He knows I struggle waiting in the silence
I want the secrets He alone can reveal
He reaches out and takes my hand
His touch is calming and I can rest
I know He will do as He has promised
But the hour is not yet at hand
He reassures me: He has not forgotten
He is growing my faith; I understand
He reminds me that we have been here before
He shows me the path lit just for me
I will not be traveling alone
He goes before me every step of the journey

As I long for home
He assures me; He wants that too
Today, He still has a purpose
I need to stay; to carry forth His plan
His children stand in need of intercession
He has called me to stand in the gap
I surely don't want to disappoint Him
He tells me I never have
I'm in awe this all started with just a baby
Yet he has always been a full-grown man
I shut the books and blow out the candles
I return to the Stillness of the Night
So honored to know what this feels like
To be loved, cherished and chosen
One day I pray I will hear it
Well done; You've led an excellent life

The busier we become the more we need to set time aside to do those things that will last for all eternity. The key to finding time to do those things we say are important to us is prioritizing. Priorities are not led by my feelings but on what I prioritize.

There will always be a to do list a mile long. Especially surrounding the holidays, the list is endless. At some point, we Get To choose what is MOST important to us.

If we do not take the time to be with Jesus, it is because He is not our first priority. If He is not the number one priority, He will always be put down the list. It is tempting to do just one or two things before spending time with Him. Before we know it, we have gone through the entire day without spending any time with him, and as the dark of night comes, we find ourselves exhausted.

"Seek the Kingdom of God above everything else and live righteously and he will give you everything you need." Matthew 6:33

This promise in Isaiah can be our daily reality and bring us so much balance and joy this Christmas. We Get To decide who provides our strength. We Get To show our family where our inner help comes from.

"You will go out in joy and be lead forth in Peace." Isaiah 55:12

Dear Jesus,

I love you. I know what I long to do but so often do not do it. Please help me run from the temptation to put so many other trivial things before my time with you. Help me just get started, and know once I do, you will more than meet me halfway. Give me a peace in those times that gives my heart, mind and soul deeper longing for time with just you and me. Help me hear your voice. Help me feel your Peace, help me have the joy that comes from you. I release all the plans I am making and ask you to help me know what you desire for me and my family today. Lord, let my choices reflect a heart that longs for you and a spirit led disposition that shines your love for all those I am with today. Help me to be what You created me to be.

In Jesus' name,

Amen

Today I am grateful for: _____   _____

_____

Today I Get To: _____

_____
_____
_____
_____
_____
_____
_____
_____

Homemade Gifts

WE ALL HAVE VIVID MEMORIES of gifts we made as children. How excited we were for our mom or dad to open our special gift. Then there are the special gifts our children make. I can still see the kids coming in the house as Christmas break was about to begin. The special gifts they had made were either wrapped or placed in a paper bag all done up with Christmas art. They would get tucked beneath the tree and we would OOH and AAH over the treasures that were within those special packages.

One year when things were very tight, my husband spent time in shop class making me a special string art picture. With basketball and everything that always crowded out that time of year for him, that made the time he took to make that for me even more special.

My sisters and I would exchange small gifts too, and on the years when the gifts were to be homemade, those are the ones we each treasured for many years to come. There were years when I tried my hand at different crafts and always enjoyed giving homemade gifts to my family. The time and energy and love that goes into those one of a kind special gifts really do mean so much to the one receiving the gift. We use our imagination, our hands, our time, our resources. We may, at times need to use all of the senses in order to create just the right gift.

I think of where this longing in each of us to be creative comes from, and I believe since we are made in the image of our heavenly Father, it comes directly from Him.

"In the beginning God created the heavens and the earth." Genesis 1:1

I have a sister that is so talented. She makes beautiful pottery and whenever anyone is fortunate enough to receive one or more of her pieces, we feel very blessed. We know the hours and meticulous care she puts into each piece. She has a vision and specific purpose for each piece. I also have family that knits. They work out each stitch with delicate detail, and at the beginning no one can tell what it will be, but once it is finished we have beautiful delicate needle points and afghans that tell stories for generations.

How much more attention to detail must God place upon each of us as He knows exactly who He is creating and the unique purpose He has created us for.

"But now, O Lord, you are our Father; we are the clay, and you are the potter; and we are all the work of your hands." Isaiah 64:8

"You made all the delicate, inner parts of my body and knit me together in my mother's womb. I praise You because I am fearfully and wonderfully made; Your works are wonderful, I know that full well. Psalm 139:13-14

In a world where there is airbrushing and plastic surgeries available to anyone at any age, it is hard to look in the mirror and be okay with what we see. I am just like many women who want to look nice and stay attractive, and I am grateful for natural products to help me age gracefully. With God's help, I desire to be a woman with His beauty coming from within me. I desire to have a quiet and gentle spirit. I want to have so much inner beauty that my outer shell isn't what people are attracted to.

We Get To decide each day to come to Jesus where His truth can be found. The more time we spend with Him, the one who created us, the more we will see the inner beauty He placed in us.

I cannot imagine opening any one of the special homemade gifts that was given to me and saying, "This isn't good enough. I wanted it to be different, something else. I want what that other person has." It isn't wrong to take care of yourself, but when we become obsessive, spending monies we do not have to add this or that to our looks, we need to reevaluate why we are so obsessed with our looks. Why don't we love and appreciate how God created us? Why don't we consider ourselves one of His masterpieces?

Today, if we choose to, We Get To look in the mirror and begin a new journey of being grateful for who He has made us to be.

We Get To work on our inner beauty so it will soon overshadow any outward flaws you think you have.

What a beautiful gift to give yourself this Christmas.

Dear Father God, Creator of all good things,

I ask you today to help me see myself through your eyes. Lord, help me begin to love myself. Help me to begin valuing what you value. Help me to have an inner beauty that will far surpass any outward flaws I still see. Thank you.

In Jesus' name,

Amen

Today I am Grateful for: _____   _____

_____

Today I Get To: _____

_____

_____

_____

_____

_____

_____

_____

_____

_____

_____

_____

DECEMBER 9

The Bell Ringers

THERE IS SOMETHING IN ME that causes me to PAUSE when I see one of the faithful Salvation Army Bell ringers. They appear every year in front of the grocery stores and local establishments as if to Ring in the Christmas season.

What causes me to pause is this: I see servant hearts willingly giving of their precious time. The conditions aren't always perfect. It can be cold, wet, hot or windy depending on where they live. And people can be not so nice this time of year—can we agree?!

I PAUSE and ask myself: What have I given today? Have I invested in anyone's life? Have I stopped what I am doing to serve someone else? Am I showing, like these who Ring the Bells, that I want my life to be about serving others? Since this season is because of Jesus Christ, should I not give consideration to what He would do?

"For even the Son of Man did not come to be served, but to serve and give His life as a ransom for many." Mark 10:45

I am also moved by each of those Bell Ringers' sweet spirits. They never make me feel guilty as I pass by. Regardless of whether I place something into their red can or not, I'm always greeted with a smile and wished a blessed day.

When I see selfless acts from such kind souls I whisper this over them as a prayer to God:

May the Lord smile on you and be gracious to you." Numbers 6:25

We Get To look for these simple, yet profound, reminders throughout our day and realign our schedule for that day. These are a few of the things I might hear during one of these PAUSE moments: "Cindy, the tone in your voice was a bit harsh this morning, you need to apologize; Cindy, you forgot that you were going to check in on your friend. You didn't reach out and check on those going through crazy health battles right now either, send out that card and let them know you are praying for them."

We all have two choices when we have those PAUSE moments. We Get To rearrange our schedules to get those important, caring acts of love done OR decide to ignore those voices and carry on with our own agenda. We cannot do everything and we women carry enough guilt around. So how do we decide what to prioritize with so many demands on our time?

When we choose to begin our day with Jesus, He will be faithful to help us decide what are the best plans for each day, one day at a time. There is a great gift we forfeit by not taking this time to sit with Him. HIS PEACE!

"Don't worry about anything; instead, pray about everything; tell God your needs and don't forget to thank Him for His answers. If you do this, you will experience God's peace, which is far more wonderful than the human mind can understand. His peace will keep your thoughts and your hearts quiet at rest as you trust in Christ Jesus." Philippians 4:6-7

Perhaps you have never taken time to just simply sit with Jesus with no agenda other than to just be together. You may not even know where to begin.

Choose one of the scriptures from each day's devotional and ask God,

"Lord, what do you want to say to me?" then just sit and listen.

Write down what you hear. It is good to look back and see how faithful He is to meet you during these quiet times. I used to hear others say how God said this or that to them and I thought, "God doesn't talk like that to me" until I began writing down anything I thought was His voice. I was literally amazed how He had been talking to me all along. It's like having a conversation with a close friend who knows everything about you, only even better. Everything He tells me is completely true and He knows even more about me than I do.

"You have made known to me the path of life; you will fill me with joy in your presence." Acts 2:28

I love this scripture. It is one I go to daily. I say I want my life to have purpose and that regardless of what the day brings, I want people to see the strength and joy of the Lord through me. What this verse reestablishes for me is the boundary lines. To achieve what I desire, I Get To spend time in His presence.

I think most of you would say you want this in your life too. We all want to leave a lasting legacy once our time on this earth is done. For people to remember what our lives stood for.

Dear Lord,

Thank you for those little reminders that help me keep staying on the path you have for me. I want to be such a shining light of your love and joy during this Christmas season. Remind me and help me to do those things you lay on my heart to serve your other children. Thank you for being the best gift anyone could ever receive.

In Jesus' precious name,

Amen

Today I am grateful for: _____   _____

_____

Today I Get To: _____

_____

_____

_____

_____

_____

Heart Transformation

~

MANY OF US KNOW MANY pieces of information about Jesus. We have formed opinions about who God is based on books we have read and what we have heard men with biblical knowledge share. There is a big shift that happens when we begin to be stirred in our spirits to really know for ourselves who this Jesus is, and even more importantly, who He is to me.

As I began doing Bible studies, I began to realize that some of the things I thought I knew about God were not based in truth. The truth was available to me for years. It was in front me each day. God's Word, the Bible, is the source of knowing truth versus man's opinion. And even greater still is the power to discern what His word is saying by asking Him to give His wisdom to discern the difference between opinion and fact.

Many of us who grew up in the church rely way too heavily upon what our pastor, priest or other clergymen taught us without testing it to see if it lined up with God's word.

"So, here's what I want you to do, God helping you: Take your everyday, ordinary life-your sleeping, eating, going to work, and walking around life – and place it before God as an offering. Embracing what God does for you is the best thing you can do for Him. Don't become so well adjusted to your culture that you fit in without even thinking. Instead, fix your attention on God. You'll be changed from the inside out. Readily recognize what He wants from you, and quickly respond to it. Unlike the culture around

you, always dragging you down to its level of immaturity, God brings the best out of you, develops well-formed maturity in you." Romans 12:1-2 The Message

We can easily get bogged down in theology, which does not yield a supernatural lifestyle. This is when information about Jesus can become a distraction, preventing us from representing Jesus.

I often pray, "Lord, help me enhance your reputation today." But I won't do this very well if I do not know who Jesus really is. The way I have separated information from truth is by spending the quiet times with Him. opening His word and allowing it to change the very core of what I believe.

"Keep on being obedient to the Word, and not merely being hearers who deceive themselves." James 1:22

When I consider the birth of Jesus I believe He knew just how much our hearts needed to be transformed by having His Holy spirit in us to guide and direct us.

He created us and knows how we are wired. Who better to help us sift through all the chaos this world places in front of us every day? We are being bombarded by media and the social network every minute of the day. And for many of us, it is one the hardest things to separate ourselves from.

We know it is ruling our time yet to set it down is a very real struggle. I believe we fear missing out and so we are glued to it, yet what is really happening is that it is causing us to miss out on the greatest One life has offered us.

God relentlessly pursues us, and I am so grateful that He does. I have had many "do overs" when I fall to the temptation to pick up my phone and bring it with me to the quiet time. I have to discipline my mind to leave it. I need to have Him transform my heart and mind each day to even stand a chance to making the best choices each day.

I Get To say no to the lesser things this world has to offer and in return, have no regrets. I Get To know that saying yes to time with Jesus is the greatest "Yes" in all the world.

Dear Lord,

Thank you for what you have done in my life to completely transform my heart. I know there is still so much to learn about who You are. Please continue to direct my mind to understanding. Also help me take what I learn about you and share how it has personally affected me. You have created me for a unique purpose. Thank you.

In Jesus' precious name,

Amen

Today I am grateful for: _____   _____

_____

Today I Get To: _____

_____

_____

_____

_____

_____

_____

_____

_____

_____

_____

_____

_____

_____

_____

_____

_____

_____

_____

No Room at the Inn

IT IS WORTH CONSIDERING WHY God would include the details of Bethlehem having no room anywhere for Mary to give birth to the Son of God. I believe there are some great lessons for us to uncover by examining the scriptures and asking God to help us understand the meaning behind why He included these details. I believe He is intentional about what he has placed in His Word.

"At that time the Roman emperor, Augustus, decreed that a census should be taken throughout the Roman Empire. This was the first census taken when Quirinius was governor of Syria. All returned to their own ancestral towns to register for this census. And because Joseph was a descendant of King David, he had to go to Bethlehem in Judea, David's ancient home. He traveled there from the village of Nazareth in Galilee. He took with him Mary, to whom he was engaged, who was now expecting a child. And while they were there, the time came for her baby to be born. She gave birth to her firstborn son. She wrapped him snugly in strips of cloth and laid Him in a manger, because there was no lodging available for them." Luke 2:1-8

Bethlehem was home to the Jews. They had been awaiting a Savior, their Messiah, for a very long time. Yet when it was finally time, Jesus' chosen people were not ready for Him. And they were really caught off guard, even offended that He came as a defenseless baby.

How often have we had "NO ROOM" in our day, week, month, or even longer for the Lord. We know He will be there to meet us, that He is the answer to the things we pray for. We go about our lives without Him. We attend church and from the outside, it looks like we are close to Jesus. But in reality, since we are not spending time with Him, we are not. He's always there but often ignored.

Before I really knew who God was, I would pray. But I'd often be caught off guard because Jesus didn't answer my prayer like I thought He would. He also had a completely different time table for when He chose to do things. I wonder if you have ever been like me? Have you been left wondering and questioning God? When life gets hard, when the trials of life seem to go on for such a long time. When you see others getting answers to their cries but you are left to continue to wait on the Lord-does it leave you wondering?

When I finally chose to take a look at myself and my relationship with Him things began to really change. We can have all the knowledge of God without it effecting our hearts. I went from blaming and questioning God to trusting Him more by simply getting to know Him, and you can too.

We will discover how much He unconditionally loves us even before we loved Him. That He thinks about us ALL the time. That He has chosen us.

He had stayed faithful to us and all of His promises even when we were not faithful to Him.

"How precious to me are your thoughts, God. How vast the sum of them, if I were to count them they would outnumber the grains of sand. When I awaken I am still with you." Psalm 139: 17-18

"You did not choose me, but I chose you. I have appointed you to go and produce fruit that will last, so that whatever you ask the Father in my name, He will give you." John 15:16

"The Lord's lovingkindness indeed never ceases, For His compassions never fail. They are new every morning; Great is Your faithfulness." Lamentations 3:22-23

The other things that help keep us grounded during this insanely busy season is considering how Mary and Joseph took what was available. They embraced the place God prepared for them. They were content even in less than sanitary conditions.

What we can learn is to stop getting upset when things don't turn out like we hoped. Entrust the unmet expectations to the One who knows what each day holds for us.

"You saw me before I was born. Every day of my life was recorded in your book. Every moment was laid out before a single day passed." Psalm 139:16

God knew where Jesus would be born. He knew the town and the exact location.

May our lives grow so aware of God's attention over the details of our lives that when things this Christmas don't go perfectly in alignment with what we thought would be happening, we realize We Get To celebrate Him laying that day out in advance and We Get To give Him praise in all things.

Dear Jesus,

Thank you for helping me make room for you today. I am grateful you love me so much. Please continue to show me how faithful and wonderful you are. Continue to help me grasp the true depth of love you have for me.

In Jesus' name,

Amen

Today I am grateful for: _____   _____

_____

Today I Get To: _____

_____

_____

_____

_____

_____

_____

DECEMBER 12
The Wise Men

THE 3 WISE MEN ARE always a part of the Christmas scene. Whether we are watching a children's program at church or at a live nativity, you can be certain to find the Magi as an integral part of the scene.

It's interesting to note that wise men in this time of history, traveled in caravans, and were associated with great wealth and prestige. These wise men studied the science of astrology and had been tracking this unusual star for over 2 years. I find it so interesting that long before we see what God is up to, he is working behind the scene prior to unveiling His work.

"Jesus Christ is the same yesterday, today and forever." Hebrews 13:8
With the three wise men came three gifts.

"And when they had come into the stable, they saw a young child with Mary His mother, and fell down and worshipped Him. And when they had opened their treasures, they presented gifts to Him; gold, frankincense, and myrrh." Matthew 2:11

When I have had to choose the perfect and fitting gift for someone with prestige it can be daunting. I want to get them something that will be honoring to them. I found it insightful to study what each of the gifts brought to Jesus represented from the Magi's perspective and from God's.

The first gift was **Gold:** It is valuable and represents royalty for kingships. It is long lasting and is a precious metal, just to name a few.

Of course, Jesus is the King of Kings and is eternal.

"And on His robe and on His thigh, He has a name written, "KING OF KINGS, AND LORD OF LORDS." Revelation 19:16
"I am the Alpha and Omega," says the Lord God, "who is, and who was and who is to come, the Almighty." Revelation 1:8

The second gift was **Frankincense:** It is a costly perfume and a symbol of a priestly role.

"For we do not have a high priest who is unable to empathize with our weaknesses, but we have one who has been tempted in every way, just as we are – yet did not sin." Hebrews 4:15

The third gift was **Myrrh:** This was used at that time as anointing oil and also for embalming. It was costly as well.

We know when Jesus' body was taken off the cross the ladies who followed Him were allowed to prepare His body for burial. They most likely would have used Myrrh.

All three of these gifts were available or grown in that region – and would have been highly sought-after gifts. Isn't it interesting to consider that while God planned for His son to be born in a lowly manger, He also wanted his son's position and future foretold through the gifts the Wise men brought?

Today we Get To be very particular about the choosing of our gifts. We Get To allow our gifts to have messages attached. Generally, what I give to my family and closest friends are more personal than other gifts that I buy. You can most likely identify with this same truth. We want the gift to say how much we love the recipient, and we want what we choose for them to be specific to their taste and character. I love meditating on these three gifts and allow them to stir in me the desire to choose just the right gifts that will be a blessing for years to come.

Dear Father God,

Just like you chose what gifts the wise men would bring your one and only Son, may I also choose wisely the gifts I Get To... give to those I love so much. Help me consider what gift I can give you today. Help my gifts be thoughtful and full of love. May you also remind me to be content wherever my day takes me and to give thanks in all things for it brings you honor and glory. I love you.

In Jesus' name,

Amen

Today I am Grateful for: _____   _____

_____

Today I Get To: _____

_____

_____

_____

_____

_____

_____

_____

_____

_____

_____

_____

_____

_____

_____

_____

_____

_____

_____

_____

_____

A Cup of Christmas Tea

WHETHER YOU'RE A COFFEE OR tea drinker, there's something quite special and relaxing about a cup of tea. Better yet is a cup enjoyed with a special friend.

One of my favorite memories is the occasional trip to a little tea room in a rural town in Michigan. To sneak off for an afternoon and enjoy a special lunch with wonderful teapots steaming with Prince of Wales tea is a memory that still brings me great joy. The teapots and fine china were eclectic and one of a kind. I imagine most of them were treasures found at antique shops. There was always a small vase of flowers on the tables adorned with fine linen from days gone by.

What made it most memorable was going there with one of my best friends. It was like taking a step back in time where all day to day pressures would be left at the door. We would sit for as long as time would allow and just chat the afternoon away.

Later, as this little tea room closed its doors, my friend and I began hosting an annual tea. Sometimes it was a spring or fall tea, but occasionally we held a Christmas tea. To be able to give the gift of "time standing still" to a few close friends was something we wanted to share. We would take great delight in choosing just the right menu. The table was decorated with old lace linens given to us by our mothers or grandmothers. We would choose little gifts for each guest to take with them to remind them of the special afternoon together. But our favorite thing to do was to go around the table and share a special memory or something the Lord had recently taught us.

A cup of tea can open up our spirits and we feel free to share our inner thoughts and dreams.

This little poem was often made into a book marker and shared with our friends.

Tea Maker
Steeped in His Word
Infused with His love
Sweetened by His Spirit
Stirred from above!

The warmth and peaceful feelings that can come from a simple cup of tea can be eternally replaced by God's Word, His Love, and His Spirit that all comes from above!

I have found that while the world tries to get us to follow the crowd, God calls me to be different. He has created each of us to be unique, one of a kind. Much like those tea cups.

What the world may not find useful any longer – God sees as a treasure.

He still has a purpose for us and finds us beautiful. Unlike us scavenging through antique shops looking for what others have considered of little worth, God knows exactly where we are. He has paid a great price. So great is His love for us, it is the only thing God calls IMMEASUREABLE!

"For as high as the heavens are above the earth, so great is His love for those who fear Him." Psalm 103:11

I consider how He knows exactly how many stars are in the sky. He knows the number of grains of sand. He has the exact distance between the Sun and the Moon and knows how fast they need to travel. Considering all this is perfectly measured out leaves me speechless when I try to put into words how humbling it is to consider that He cannot measure His love for us.

While you are spending this time alone with Jesus consider the words of the poem. Let those words wash over you and truly become your reality.

There's nothing quite like having a cup of tea with Jesus.

Dear Jesus,

Thank you for the gift of simple pleasures like a cup of tea. Lord, as I sit with you today, may you infuse me with your love and sweeten me with your spirit. Lord, please show me how to bless my friends this Christmas season. Help me slow down and really enjoy the moments set apart for quiet reflection. May all I do and say be pleasing to you today.

In Jesus' name,

Amen

Today I am grateful for: _____   _____

_____

Today I Get To: _____

_____

_____

_____

_____

_____

_____

_____

_____

_____

_____

_____

DECEMBER 14

Starry, Starry Night

⌒

ONE OF MY FONDEST CHRISTMAS childhood memories is when my mother would load me and my sisters in the car and we would go in search of the beautifully decorated homes. The snow would crunch under our boots at the crisp cold frozen ground. The sky would be filled with so many stars and we would look up in search of the big and little dipper.

We would sing Christmas carols and OOH and AAH at how the lights would glisten over the freshly fallen snow. My mother found ways to bring the magical traditions of Christmas alive without it costing her more than a little bit of gas.

There is another group that had the beautiful night sky over their heads that first Christmas. They were ordinary men but chosen by God to be included in the glad news of the Christ child being born. Interesting that they were chosen and God knew they would believe the news.

"That night there were shepherds staying in the fields nearby, guarding their flocks of sheep. Suddenly, an angel of the Lord appeared among them, and the radiance of the Lord's Glory surrounded them. They were terrified, but the angel reassured them. "don't be afraid!" he said. "I bring you good news that will bring great joy to all people. The Savior – yes, the Messiah, The Lord – has been born today in Bethlehem, the city of David! And you will recognize him by this sign: You will find a baby wrapped in snugly strips of cloth, lying in a manger."

"When the angels had returned to Heaven the shepherds said to each other, "Let's go to Bethlehem! Let's see this thing that has happened, which the Lord has told us about." Luke 2: 8-12, 15

There is something about the beauty of creation, like a star filled night that speaks volumes about the truth of God being who He says He is.

Can you imagine with me what the shepherds must have felt on that blessed night of the Christ child's birth? Imagine the fear that gripped them when the angel appeared to them. Yet, even more amazing is to consider - even in their fear, they trusted completely in the Word of God.

As we sit quietly before the Lord each morning, seeking Him to share with us the good news, we too will find Christ in a deeply intimate and personal way. Like He did with the shepherds, I believe God wants to share special things with us as well.

"Call to me and I will answer you and tell you great and unsearchable things you do not know." Jerimiah 33:3

During this Christmas season let's remember it is a time of Advent, a time to prepare for something coming. The birth of Jesus happened over 2,000 years ago and He came to share His life with us. To make a way because apart from Him coming, there was no way.

"God will make a way where there seems to be no way." Isaiah 43:16

If your Christmases have often been filled with stress from the world's heavy demands, may I remind you that His ways are so much different than the world's.

He desires for us to come and rest with Him, and when He is the Reason for the Season, then we will find it easier to lay down our burdened life and pick up only what He is asking us to.

Like those shepherds watching their flocks by night, free from all the noise that would have otherwise made it hard to be prepared to hear the angel's news, we Get To set aside the noise for a few brief moments and enjoy the quiet peaceful presence of the same Jesus the shepherds traveled to Bethlehem to see.

The lyrics of an old hymn serves as a great reminder that this Christmas, we Get To spend time with our friend Jesus.

"Oh, what peace we often forfeit,
oh, what needless pain we bear.
All because we do not carry,
everything to God in prayer."

Dear Jesus,

Oh, how grateful I am for those quiet beautiful starry nights. Remind me this Christmas to look up and gaze with wonder into your creation. To know that you have things you want to share with me. Increase my desire to spend quiet, intimate time with you in prayer and not forfeit the peace you promise to give me. Guide me each day to only take on what you have for me and to trust you with the remainder of the things on my to-do-list. I am believing you are my Peace.

In Jesus' name,

Amen

Today I am Grateful for: _____   _____

_____

Today I Get To: _____

_____

_____

_____

_____

_____

_____

_____

_____

Holiday Baking

I THINK WE ALL HAVE those special childhood memories that include stirring up a batch of Christmas cookies or some other family recipe that is just a special part of our holiday traditions. The kitchen is full of Christmas spirit as the ingredients are pulled out of cupboards and the special cookie cutters are placed on the counter. The laughter and joy that fills the air in anticipation of doing a fun family baking project together is unique in and of itself. Adding to the making of new memories is the awareness that our families have been baking these special recipes for generations. Oh, to hear the compliment when someone says, "they taste just like our mom's or grandmother's."

So often the baking projects in our homes are done by just one, so the time of coming together, sneaking bites of the yummy dough and discussing exactly how we are going to add our own personal style to decorating our stack of cookies is to be treasured. Yes, it can get messy, but what a good messy, the way the flour and cookie decorations are spread out across the kitchen counter or island with plenty making its way to the floor.

You can't just get the different ingredients from the store into your home and expect the special recipe to just get put together. There is an intentionality of the time and effort it takes to "stir up" the ingredients in just the right order. It is time consuming and with so many things on our to do list, we have to make this a priority if it is something we want to get done.

As I was reading in 1 Timothy I was struck by something else that has to be intentionally stirred up. I also love how it was something passed on from one generation to the next.

"I remember your genuine faith, for you share the faith that first filled your grandmother Lois and your mother, Eunice. And I know that same faith continues strong in you. This is why I remind you to stir up the gift of God which is in you through the laying on of my hands." 2 Timothy 1:5-6

Some of us have a rich legacy of faithful saints that have gone before us, while for some others, you may be the first one in your family to leave this imprint of strong faith.

Just as Paul was encouraging Timothy to stay on the path his mother and grandmother were known for; I want to encourage you to be the light in your homes and families. I guarantee you, Lois and Eunice struggled daily to set their feet to the path God had for them. We all have to keep our eyes on Jesus in order to be able to walk in the spirit.

"Keep your eyes on Jesus, who both began and finished this race we're in. Study how He did it. Because He never lost sight of where He was headed – that exhilarating finish in and with God – He could put up with anything along the way: cross, shame, whatever. And now He's there, in the place of honor, right alongside God." Hebrews 12:2

I love how no matter what your day holds, there are scriptures to remind us that the time invested in growing our faith effects every area, including baking.

This Christmas, as you are stirring up your batch of goodies, pause and let yourself consider how you can Stir Up the faith that is already in you.

"Oh, taste and see the Lord is good; Blessed is the man who trusts n Him." Psalm 34:8

Here are a few suggestions to help you Stir Up your faith:

Good Bible studies with accountability partners can help you stay disciplined to do your time with the Lord. Be very intentional when choosing who you are spending time with because we are all listening to someone.

First: Ask God His plans and perspective in each part of our day, all day long. Being in God's Word is a key part of this.

Second: Having sound advice from other Godly men or women will reinforce your faith building decisions. Ask God who these might be in your life.

Third: What you are feeding your mind is important. Consider the music, TV and other media choices. Be sure they are having a positive influence to Stir Up your faith.

"Above all else, guard your heart, for everything you do flows from it." Proverbs 4:23

Dear Heavenly Father,

Thank you that I Get To experience the pure joy that comes from long living family traditions. Thank you that through a simple and fun activity of baking cookies, I Get To be reminded to Stir Up my faith. Lord, I desire to make good choices today. Show me, all day long which path you have for me that will Stir Up greater faith and help me mature and become complete in you. I love you, Jesus.

In Jesus' name,

Amen

Today I Am Grateful For: _____ _____

_____

Today I Get To: _____

_____

_____

_____

_____

_____

_____

_____

DECEMBER 16

WWJD

~

It wasn't that long ago that people would ask, "What would Jesus do?"

It was a catchy phrase, but more importantly, it could cause us to reconsider our actions for any given scenario.

This Christmas let's re-think this little phrase because we are, as His children, representing God. We may very well be the only Jesus many will see. While none of us can quite model hosting the Presence of God more effectively than Jesus, we can, with God's help, be a light in a very dark world. We can love, serve, feed, clothe, encourage, speak life into someone every day.

"Lord, when did we ever see you hungry or thirsty or a stranger, or without clothing or sick or in prison and not help you? And God answered, "I tell you the truth, whatever you do unto the least of these you do unto me." Matthew 25: 44-45

"All of you together are Christ's body, and each of you are part of it." 1 Corinthians 12:27

I don't think anyone can deny that the world is in search of "something more". Rick Warren's book, *The Purpose Driven Life*, would not have sold over 30 million copies if this were not true. At one time or another, most of us wonder if we are doing what we were made to do.

With certainty, we are called to represent Jesus while we are here on this earth. The weight of our daily purpose can be sobering and yet it is so rewarding to impact our world for all eternity. To know that Jesus chose us to carry on His work through us is humbling. We may not feel qualified to do this. It becomes even more important to learn how He walked this earth and follow His example.

Jesus was every bit a man while He was here on earth. He was tempted in every way. He had sisters and brothers that were not always supportive. He was prone to wander at an early age. He did manual work helping His father as a carpenter. He attended weddings with His mother.

If I am feeling discouraged I can tend to have thoughts like this, "Of course, Jesus lived a perfect life, He is God!" But the fact is that He was anointed by the Holy Spirit, and that is why He lived a perfect life in the midst of life here on earth. We too, as children of God are anointed. We have the Holy Spirit living in us.

For many of us, our greatest points of weakness will hit when we are tired. Our schedules are already overloaded. But then add the unique demands of the Christmas season and we have to be extra intentional to give our bodies the care it needs so it can operate like God intended. The most important thing that messes up my heart, mind, body and soul is when I neglect to spend time with God. This time with God has become my first priority above everything else. I allow His spirit to renew my mind, my heart, my soul.

As I do this, a passion and purpose wells up within me. It gives me energy for the day. God's supernatural resources go beyond anything this world can provide and spills over into my family and others throughout the course of the day. Our world and the culture of this age desperately need what we have. The key is sitting quietly with God before your day begins. I honestly cannot adequately describe what the investment of this time will bring into your life. It is something that you just have to have the faith and desire to try. I promise you, it will completely change the way you interact with others. You will have a greater peace and strength to handle the demands of your day.

My prayer is that each of us, in committing this time each morning, will be blown away with how Jesus shows up and the unique blessings He brings all throughout our days.

The power that shows up in us who have spent time with Him is what will show the world "What Jesus Would do!"

"I tell you the truth, anyone who believes in me will do the same works I have done, and even greater works, because I am going to be with the Father. You can ask for anything in my name and I will do it so that the Son can bring glory to the Father. Yes, ask for anything in my name and I will do it." John 14: 12-14

Dear Holy Spirit,

I invite you in to saturate every part of my life. You are the only one who can bring purpose to every part of my day. Help me enhance your reputation today. Let me love, serve, feed, extend a helpful hand and be ready to be your hands and feet to anyone I see in need today. Remind me in the busyness of my day that I may be the only Jesus people see.

In Jesus' name,

Amen

Today I am grateful for: _____   _____

Today I Get To: _____

_____

_____

_____

_____

_____

_____

_____

_____

Countdown to Christmas

DON'T YOU JUST LOVE IT when you hear in the middle of summer, this many weeks left before Christmas? Or as the beauty of Fall is upon us they begin tearing down the Fall decorations so that the Christmas trees and all that glitters fills the malls and shopping centers before November 1 is even here? It seems the marketing of Christmas is pushed up a little bit more each year. We all know if the media can cause our minds to feel the panic of "tick tock.... tick tock…" the time is running out, we will rush to spend money before it is necessary.

All year long we are waiting for the time when our lives won't be so busy and rushed. When we can look at our calendars and not have a panic attack. Since this is most likely not going to happen any time soon let's look for another approach to enjoy each day, one day at a time.

Seems like the theme of many of the previous days, and the ones to follow speak of how crazy our schedules are and how we can continue to deceive ourselves into thinking, "When this part of my life calms down, I will begin doing…" It is an illusion and one the devil uses to keep us from the very best things God has in store for us. He is waiting for us. And God will continue to wait, but why should we waste another day putting off until tomorrow the blessing He has in store for us today?

"The thief's purpose is to steal, kill and destroy. My purpose is to give them a rich and satisfying life." John 10: 10

It can be so easy to put things off. We plan on doing something, we have good intentions, but we talk ourselves out of starting today. We have all heard the saying, we put off until tomorrow knowing tomorrow never comes. Thinking of adding something new to your life during Christmas might appear to be crazy. So much of what we get bogged down in during the holidays pulls us farther away from the true meaning of Christmas: The Christ Child and celebrating His birth. We can say, "This Christmas I am going to spend time with Jesus." Again, that one day will not come without removing some of the clutter from our calendars and committing to no more delays.

Listen to the longing for God's blessing in the inner battle going on in David's psalm:

"LORD you are mine! I promise to obey Your words! With all my heart, I want Your blessings. Be merciful as You have promised. I ponder the direction of my life, and I turned to follow Your laws. I will hurry, without delay, to obey Your commands. Evil people try to drag me into sin, but I am firmly anchored to Your instructions. I rise at midnight to thank You for Your just regulations. I am a friend to anyone who fears You- anyone who obeys Your commandments. O LORD, Your unfailing love fills the earth; teach me your decrees." Psalm 119:57-64

We can all agree that there will always be a reason to put off spending alone time with Jesus, especially if you feel intimidated. You may feel like you don't know what to do or what to say.

Begin simply by picking up this devotional one day at a time, pray the prayers at the end of each day's entry and then just begin a conversation with Him. It may seem uncomfortable at first, however praying to Jesus is just like talking to a friend. You will notice I always say "Dear" before I add Jesus or God or Heavenly Father. If I were writing a letter to a friend that's how I would state it. It was easier when I first began praying to pray by writing down my prayers and I chose to do the prayers in letter format. It kept me focused on our talk, and when I want to, I can look back and see how God has been faithful to answer hundreds and thousands of my prayers. He is so faithful. I have seen that over the years and I know three things for sure. He is real, He is who He says He is and He is faithful to every one of His promises!

When you have a good friend, you know you can count on them to be flexible and understanding when we have to reschedule. They still love to be with us and they do not apply pressure to our already stressful lives. This is how Jesus is too. What he offers is a time of refreshing. He is the best friend you will ever have and time with Him will refresh your soul.

"A sweet friendship refreshes the soul." Proverbs 27:9

Dear Jesus,

Thank you that your purpose is to give me a rich and satisfying life. So often I forfeit my time with you and I know you are still merciful to me. Help me think about the direction You want for me. Help me make it a priority to follow your ways. I ask you to keep pursuing me and teaching me your ways. Lord I am grateful for your refreshing friendship.

In Jesus' precious name,

Amen

Today I am Grateful For: _____   _____

_____

Today I Get To: _____

_____

_____

_____

_____

_____

Fan Club

MOST OF US HAVE ATTENDED a concert. Depending on who the headliner is determines how crazy the crowd can be. These days the ticket sales can go for a high price and still sell out in record time. These fans are known to follow these stars from location to location. Let's explore a couple examples of those who have big fan clubs.

Recently, my son took his two sisters to an Adele concert. I should also mention he took them to Dublin for this experience and upgraded so they could enjoy this as VIPs. Let's just say he definitely won the "BEST BROTHER" award!

I asked my son what was included with this VIP ticket. They had a nice dinner before and then had up close seating but…they actually stood for the whole concert. Just seeing pictures of them as Adele began singing spoke volumes. There were several in the group crying and really being moved by the whole opportunity to see her perform live.

The other example I'll share is from the 1960's. It was a time when "BEATLE MANIA" was everywhere. These four young men from across the pond literally changed the face of music. People would scream and cry, faint and throw things on stage, and…well, you get the idea. It was pure mania! Their concerts were sold out then, and while the Beatles broke up years ago, there are still millions of Beatle fans.

Interesting to note that Adele isn't touring now and may not ever again and certainly the Beatles' time has come and gone.

But with all this, we can't forget Santa. His popularity has stood the test of time. While the need to sit on his lap only lasts a few years, it is still something parents stand in long lines for.

It is important to understand that the power in the Kingdom of God is in the form of a person as well. Let me take you to a scene where the streets were crowded with people who are eager for a glimpse and to just get near to The Man who had become so famous for wonderful things. This man had raised the dead, healed the sick, drove out demons, made the blind see and the lame walk. He had become the single focus of the entire town. People (fans) followed Jesus everywhere.

Now, you know if you've ever been in a crowd, the people are pushing and shoving. There isn't much tolerance for someone trying to get ahead of the crowd. On one such day there was a desperate woman who saw her chance for a miracle. She had carried her affliction for many years without any hope of recovery. At her own risk, she presses into the crowd so that she can reach out and touch the edge of Jesus' clothing. She doesn't want to draw attention to herself. She is too much of an outcast to embarrass herself by talking to him or to get His attention.

"Now a woman, having a flow of blood for twelve years, who had spent all her livelihood on physicians and could not be healed by any, came from behind and touched the border of His garment. And immediately her flow of blood stopped. And Jesus said, "Who has touched me?" When all denied it, Peter and those with Him said, "Master, the multitudes throng and are pressing you, and you say, "Who touched Me?" But Jesus said, "Somebody touched Me, for I perceived power going out from Me." Now when the woman saw that she was not hidden, she came trembling; and falling down before Him, she declared to Him in the presence of all people the reason she had touched Him and how she was healed immediately. And He said to her, "Daughter, be of good cheer; your faith has made you well! Go in peace." Luke 8:43-48

I have never thought of myself as a Fan Club person until I consider how many fans Jesus had. They literally followed Him from town to town, they pushed and shoved and pressed in just to get near to Him. Some were like this woman, they were desperate for healing. He was their last hope. Others wanted to see who was this man who proclaimed to be the Son of God. Some just came to see the wonders and miracles and left seeing but not knowing who this man was.

Today is no different, we can go to church, listen to sermons and read great books without accepting Jesus as our one true and lasting hope and Savior; we will have seen and heard but left not knowing Jesus.

A personal relationship with Jesus is available to anyone. Unlike the stars we throng to and pay big money to see. Jesus paid the price of your ticket to sit with him, eat with Him and be friends with Him. He wants nothing more than for you and Him to spend eternity together. He will move you to your very core, and Jesus will never be a person of the past.

"Jesus is the same yesterday, today and forever." Hebrews 13:8

Dear Lord and Savior,

Today, I want to receive you as my Lord and Savior. I confess all my sins. I know you came as an infant, lived here on this earth and then died on the cross for me.

Lord, I thank you for this woman's example, that all I need to do is have faith and I will be healed and saved from this day forward. Thank you for the priceless gift of my salvation.

In Jesus' name,

Amen

Today I am Grateful For: _____ _____

_____

Today I Get To: _____

_____

_____

A Mother's Touch

EVEN AS A YOUNG GIRL I knew that I wanted to be a stay home mom when I grew up. My favorite year growing up was when I was just 5 years old. It was the only year my mom stayed home. I have fond memories of coming home from school to my mom waiting there. I am so grateful for that year. The very next year my mother became a single mother, and from that day forward worked hard at being the best mom a girl could ever hope to have. I think the special memories of that year fueled the desire for my desire to stay home. I have always been so grateful that my husband, Mark, supported that desire.

Let's consider Mary: she was young, unmarried and discovering she would be Jesus' mother. Imagine what that must have been like for her. She was troubled and even afraid, but not afraid to ask questions.

"Mary was greatly troubled at his words and wondered what kind of greeting this might be. How will this be, Mary asked the angel, since I am a virgin." Luke 1:29,34

She was chosen specifically, and I love that she was a willing servant even with so many unanswered questions.

"I am the Lord's servant, "Mary answered. "May it be to me as you have said." Then the angel left her." Luke 1:38

Now let's consider the calling on our lives. We each have been created for such a specific purpose. How often do we find ourselves going about our lives when, like Mary, God uncovers a path that we are not expecting? One we may not have comprehended and do not feel qualified for. Often these twists and turns are accompanied with many unanswered questions.

Timing and trust are inseparable. The more intimately we know God the more we will be able to trust Him no matter what! We move forward in blind faith.

"Now faith is the substance of things hoped for, the evidence of things not seen." Hebrews 11:1

"The Lord directs the steps of the Godly. He delights in every detail of their lives. Psalm 37:23

A Mother's touch is needed to kiss a knee and make it all better, rub a back to calm an upset child, apply a cold washcloth to bring down the fever, give a hug at just the right time, hold a hand or give a much-needed pat on the back. A Mother's touch is needed to cradle a child, rock a child to sleep, calm the fears of a bad dream and softly brush back the hair from their child's forehead. And a Mother's touch is needed to make a house a home. God values our role as Mothers.

Let's consider too, The Master's touch. When His love is allowed in to touch us, it brings Healing, Wholeness, Love, Acceptance, Forgiveness, Restoration, Peace, just to name a few. Like only a Mother's touch can soothe what's ailing, Our Heavenly Father, on a much deeper and lasting way can bring renewal to all we stand in need of. For those who do not know the love of a mother, God will be all you need.

"As a mother comforts her child, so I comfort you." Isaiah 66:13

When you hear the name Mary, you think of Jesus' mother. When people hear your name what will they remember you as? You may be at an age where you don't even know what your calling is, but you can be rest assured that God is directing that path. Every twist and turn is in the hands of God. Even the mistakes we make are in God's hands.

"Your eyes saw my unformed body; all the days ordained for me were written in your book before one of them came to be." Psalm 139:14
"And we know that in all things God works for the good of those who love Him and have been called according to His purpose." Romans 8:28

As I write this I am very aware some of you reading this want to be a mother more than the air you breathe. I won't pretend to know what you are going through and when God will answer your prayers, but I do know this. God sees you. He hears your cries. I commit to interceding on your behalf. I ask that the God of ALL power and miracles will bless you with a child.

Dear Precious Lord and Savior,

We are grateful for the gift of motherhood. We pray for wisdom to raise up our children in the grace and knowledge of you, our Lord and Savior. We lift up your daughters who long for a child to be given the desires of their hearts. Help them trust you alone to fill this longing.

In Jesus' name,
Amen

Today I am Grateful For: _____ _____
_____

Today I Get To: _____
_____
_____
_____
_____
_____
_____
_____
_____
_____
_____

DECEMBER 20

The Lifeline

~⁀

HOPEFULLY, YOU WHO ARE READING this are familiar with an old TV show called Little House on the Prairie. Every week my sisters and I would pop the popcorn and get ready for the weekly saga. The story is about the Ingalls family and is set in the 1870's.

One such week we were watching as a huge snow storm settled in over the territory. The children were let out of school early to get directly home before the visibility would become nonexistent. When some of the children went missing the men headed out in search of the children. Some of the houses had attached a rope from the house to the barns so when they had to go out to feed the animals they would be able to use the rope as a guide, without it their lives were in danger. They referred to this as a lifeline.

Just as in a snow storm, where our vision can get blurred, so can our perspective. We need a higher view. We can become so weighed down by the clutter in our lives. At Christmas time the to-do-lists are endless. There is a fine line, easily crossed when we focus too much on the petty tasks. These to-do-lists that are made to keep us organized and alleviate stress are in fact making the weight of what we are choosing to carry unbearable! Since there will always be an endless list of things we can't possibly get done, why not choose a different path.

"Give all your worries and cares to God, for He cares for you." 1 Peter 5:7

May I suggest we go to our LIFELINE first. Let God be the giver of the list. Let Him prompt our hearts to the priorities He has for each given day. Can you trust Him enough to do what He places in front of you and trust the rest for another day? We need to remember that our ultimate goal is living close to the one who gave us this day.

"This is the day that the Lord has made; Let us rejoice and be glad in it." Psalm 118:24

There was definitely a time in my life where I said I trusted Jesus, but my actions told another story. My heart was in the right place. I wanted to give my family all the special touches of Christmas and keep up on all the other things "I" felt were important. At the end of the day I could make life for those in my home miserable. We've all heard the saying; "If momma ain't happy, ain't nobody happy." It took me many years to learn to ease up and let go of some of the things that really were petty. I had to ask God to show me what He wanted and I asked Him to help me stop obsessing about things that really do not matter. I desired my life reflect a heart that rested in Him.

"Examine me, O LORD, and test me! Evaluate my inner thoughts and motives! Psalm 26:2

God is very gentle with us. He really is our friend. He wants to show us how to live a successful life. Once we begin to set some of the things down that are burdensome we can begin experiencing more joy. Our minds won't be so cluttered

We will be freed up rather than the weights holding us down. We will more clearly see His face all throughout our day. Putting some limitations on our schedules will actually bring in the ability to say yes to healthy boundaries. We just need to look up and He will provide all we need.

"I will lift up mine eyes to the mountains – where my help comes from. My help comes from the LORD, the Maker of heaven and earth." Psalm 121:1-2

"Commit your actions to the LORD, and your plans will succeed." Proverbs 16:3

There are times in life that we do all we do just because we have always done it that way. I think about an elephant. They have a chain around their ankles when they are young but when they get older only a string is needed to keep them from going anywhere. They only know learned behavior so they remain chained, when in reality there is but a mere string holding them in place.

How many times in our lives are we being held down by learned behavior? We are free in Christ but we forfeit the peace He offers us. A peace filled, unburdened life is a choice. We Get To stop comparing ourselves with this world and choose the path of Jesus. Choose to let His Peace RULE in our hearts and set aside all the stress.

"Let the peace of Christ rule in your hearts, to which indeed you were called in one body. And be thankful." Colossians 3:15

Dear Lord,

You know my schedule. You see my to-do-lists. You knit me together so you know how I battle the temptation to "do it all". Help me begin, with baby steps to set one thing down today that can wait. Show me what should even be off the list. Lord I desire to let your peace rule in me. I am exhausted from my life. I know I said yes to some things I should have said no to. Help me listen and obey your prompting. Help me not try to measure up to this world- but rather help me choose to have a quiet and gentle spirit that blesses my family and friends. I love you Lord. Thank you for caring about me enough to speak these truths over me.

In Jesus' name,

Amen

Today I am Grateful For: _____ _____

_____

Today I Get To: _____

_____

_____

_____

Nutcracker Ballet

WHILE I HAVE NEVER ACTUALLY done any ballet, I find it interesting how we can parallel some of the practices they have in order to be successful at their artistic dance.

Did you know that each time a ballerina makes a full turn she returns her eyes to the same stationary point with a quick turn of her head? She does this to avoid losing her balance. She allows the rhythm of the music to dictate how precise her movements are. She is trained to make light and graceful movements.

Whenever we are feeling a little bit off balance, we can reorient ourselves to Jesus. By abiding in Christ, we will renew our minds. Some of you may be unfamiliar with what abiding in Christ means. There is a word picture in scripture that paints a perfect portrait for us.

"Yes, I am the vine; you are the branches. Those who remain in me, and I in them, will produce much fruit. For apart from me you can do nothing." John 15:5

The vine is Jesus, while we, believers in Christ, are the branches. Jesus is the master gardener and he tends to the branches. This picture of a branch not being able to survive very long apart from the vine is exactly what our lives are like when we don't live in close relationship with Jesus. What He has is our life source. While we might think we are ok not doing life with God, the truth is we are slowly wasting away. If we want to have a life that last forever we need to abide, stay close to the Lord.

Just like the ballerina, in order to avoid losing our balance, we must keep looking to Jesus.

"Let us fix our eyes on Jesus, the author and finisher of our faith. Hebrews 12:2

As we determine to celebrate the wonder that surrounds Jesus birth in Bethlehem, let's take a few moments to think about our rebirth into eternal life. After all this is the sole purpose for Jesus leaving heaven to come down to earth.

I think of the family and friends we know who have left everything they have to go serve on the mission field. Some of them leave for years at a time and sell most of what they have to go pour out their lives as a living testimony. They do as Jesus did. They go and do life next to these people groups that the Lord has given them a heart for. They don't yet know these people, but yet they love them.

We are that people group that Jesus left everything for. He has a heart for us that we do not begin to comprehend.

"We love because He first loved us." 1 John 4:19

The closest thing most of us can identify with this kind of love is when we are pregnant with a child. The love for that child grows before we see or hold them.

But when you consider how God did form us, He knew us before we were ever born. He is the one who created us. It is somewhat easier to imagine and then accept this love.

"For you created me in my inmost being; you knit me together in my mother's womb. I praise you because I am fearfully and wonderfully made; Your works are wonderful, I know that full well. My frame was not hidden from you when I was made in the secret place, when I was woven together in the depths of the earth. Your eyes saw my unformed body." Psalm 139: 13-16

Take some time to think about how much thought God put into creating you. And then continue reading below to see how often God thinks about each of us. It is sobering. While we fill our days so full that we have to remove some demands in order to make time with God a priority; He is doing just the opposite. It completely wrecks me to know God thinks about me ALL the time. It is a good wrecking, for it helps me realign my priorities when they get out of whack.

"How precious to me are your thoughts, God. How vast the sum of them! Were I to count them, they would outnumber the grains of sand- when I awake I am still with you." Psalm 139:17-18

Dear Lord,

Thank you for all the care you put into creating me. I am humbled to realize with fresh wonder how often I am on your mind. May this truth remain fresh on my heart and give me a deeper desire to, keep my eyes on you so my attention is focused on what is best. Help me to abide in your presence and receive fresh life from you, the vine.

In Jesus' name,

Amen

Today I am Grateful For: _____   _____

_____

Today I Get To: _____

_____

_____

_____

_____

_____

_____

_____

_____

_____

_____

_____

Unshakable

Do you have anyone in your home that likes to pick up the wrapped packages and shake them? In hopes to guess what the gift might be they survey the weight, size, and sounds that might be heard as they shake the present. Sometimes, if it is breakable, there may even be "FRAGILE" or "DON'T SHAKE" written on the name tag.

We have a few of these eager, childlike family members in our home and age has nothing to do with their ability to WAIT until it is time to open the gifts. I am sure you have one or two of these in your families too. It can make it a challenge to tuck the gifts for these family members a little further in behind the tree or even keep them hidden until it almost time for the gifts to be opened.

Let's go back to the word FRAGILE. We all know someone, it may even be you, who has been through such a traumatic experience your faith has been badly bruised and perhaps even broken. You may not be sure you believe in God anymore. But if you have taken the time to read this devotional, then maybe, just maybe you're not sure if you dare trust this ONE who has allowed all this to happen in your life.

I wouldn't begin to try to give you answers to questions only God can answer. But I also would say, we live in a fallen world. It is not God who has caused these tragic events in your life. But it is only God who can use them in your life. I would also say that God can handle any questions you have for Him. He is able to carry the burden of the anger and hurt and distrust you have for Him.

I would not believe in a God who did bad things to us. I do believe in a good God who takes a personal interest in each of us. My God loves each of us so much that He sent Jesus down as a baby and then allowed him after 33 years on this earth to willingly allow His one and only Son to die for each of us. To carry our burdens to the cross.

I believe in a God who loves us more than we can imagine. I believe in a God who sees our fragile state and wants to strengthen us and help us grow to believe He is who He says He is. That He is a good, good Father.

The closer I Get To God, the more I realize just How good He is. How relentlessly He pursues each of us. I do not believe it is a coincidence that you are reading this Advent Devotional. God has allowed this little book to cross your path to bless you and direct your steps to this very place. That is relentless Love!

If you are a parent, think back to the first time you laid eyes on your child. Did they have to do anything to earn your love? No, of course not. And in some respects, it's shocking how instant the love is.

Now consider when your child has an accident that requires stiches, or when they are bullied at school. What if they are unfortunate enough to get a more serious diagnosis which requires months of doctor and hospital visits?

Now imagine your child wondering: because these tragic things have happened, if you, their parent loves them. If you can be trusted? After all, as parents we are supposed to protect them. But instead, what happens? Children have simple childlike faith. They cling to their parents. They trust them. They want them with them all the time. They know they are loved. They see it is killing you to watch them endure such hard things. They know this was not your plan for them. But we have a much more difficult time entrusting the hard stuff to God.

Our God is a loving Father. When these tragic events happen, we can push Him away, or we can run to Him. Knowing He is the one who will fight for us. He will comfort us. He will never leave us. He will Love us regardless if our fear tries to shut Him out or not.

"What shall we say about such wonderful things? If God is for us, who can be against us? And I am convinced that nothing can ever separate us from God's love. Neither death nor life, neither angels nor demons, neither our fears for today nor our worries about tomorrow-not even the powers of hell can separate us from the love of God." Romans 8:31, & 38

Love is not something God does. Love is Who God is.

"Whoever does not love does not know God, because God is Love. 1 John 4:8

"When I think of all this, I fall to my knees and pray to the Father, the Creator of everything in heaven and on earth. I pray that from His glorious, unlimited resources he will empower you with inner strength through His spirit. When Christ will make His home in your hearts as you trust Him. Your roots will grow down into God's love and keep you strong. And may you have the power to understand, as all God's people should, how wide, how long, how high, and how deep is the love of Christ, though it is too great to understand fully. Then you will be made complete with all the fullness of life and power that comes from God." Ephesians 3: 16-19

Dear Lord,

Thank you that your love is unshakable. That you are the God who is with us in our best and worst days. Lord I pray that you will give each of inner strength so our hearts, though some may be afraid to, will trust you. Help our roots grow down deep in awareness of how much you do love us and help us run to you each day knowing that while we do not know what the day holds, we know you hold it and will hold us whatever may come. Thank you for your relentless love.

In Jesus' name,

Amen

Today I am Grateful For: _____   _____

_____

Today I Get To: _____

_____

The Fire Within

~9

"Listen to me in the silence."

ISAIAH 41:1

NOW YOU MAY BELIEVE THAT silence is impossible with a house full of children, your furry friends, laughter, disputes over the remote, piano lessons and any number of other activities a buzz within the walls of your home. We love the sound of family and the memories we are unconsciously storing up. But oh, for but a few minutes of silence.

Now imagine this scene: Sitting alone in a comfy chair with feet resting on a soft ottoman. A crackling of logs in the fireplace. The freedom to take in the solitude. Being quite ok with being alone. The quiet allows you to hear sounds that you hadn't heard when all that life was happening within your home. But now, all are tucked in for the night and there is a magical silence. Peace. You can hear yourself think or be free to not have to think about anything for a few glorious moments.

Silence may be golden, but as a culture we are conditioned to avoid it, to fill all our waking moments with noise or activity. The quiet can in fact be so uncomfortable we can hardly wait to get busy again. Silence can be a very fearful thing. Silence can create an anxiety leaving one to feel empty and hollow.

"Go out and stand before me on the mountain," the Lord told him. And as Elijah stood there, the Lord passed by, and a mighty windstorm hit the mountain. It was such a terrible blast that the rocks were torn loose, but the Lord was not in the wind. After the wind there was an earthquake, but the Lord was not in the earthquake. And after the earthquake, there was a fire, but the Lord was not in the fire. And after the fire there was a sound of a gentle whisper. When Elijah heard it, he wrapped his face in his cloak and went out and stood at the entrance of the cave. 1 Kings 19:11-13

But as the scripture above suggests, Silence is the discipline by which the inner fire of God is tended and kept alive. When it is just us alone in front of the fireplace, we see the colors shooting out of the different size timbers. We hear pops and crackling that we missed when the noise of family crowded it out. We smell the embers and notice the red-hot coals. It is surprisingly amazing what wonder we miss when life is flying by at warp speed. So, it is with God, He speaks in whispers. We forfeit those moments He has carved out for us to enjoy His presence. He has things to share with us, but we have to be willing to make time for Him to speak and for us to listen. We rush the quiet away by turning on the TV, making a phone call or picking up our social media to fill a hole that it never will.

We can only hear our children breathing when we are quiet and close enough to listen. And, we can only hear God whisper when we intentionally seek moments of silence.

Christmas without music would be like Christmas without family; but Christmas without silence would be like a day without bedtime. One is as essential as another. One without the other is incomplete.

We each have an inner fire burning within us; but when we continue to look to the world to fill the inner longing, we will always come away with those deepest needs unmet. Things and other people are meant to be blessings in our lives, but when we make the mistake of allowing those blessings to keep us from knowing the one who is providing the blessing, we do ourselves a deep disservice.

Sadly, our children are learning that every minute of every day must be filled or boredom sets in. We are a society that is ran ragged.

We live for vacations that barely give us time to unplug before we have to return to the day to day routine.

God never meant for us to live such lives of exhaustion. We must begin to change the way we are managing our time and give Him the best part of our days instead of the leftovers. The enemy has convinced us to never stop. To get all you can any way you can-but in fact it steals the life we desire, kills our relationships and destroys our peace. Can you see the twisted way Satan has warped our thinking?

"My purpose is to give them a rich and satisfying life. The thief comes to steal, kill and destroy. I have come so that they may have life and have it in abundance," John 10:10

So today, watch for the moments where God is calling you into the quiet. Allow His gentle whisper to speak life into your weary bones. Enjoy the glorious moments He has carved out for you today. He has a drink of living water to give you that will keep the fire within you burning bright.

"Jesus replied, "If you only knew the gift God has for you and who you are speaking to, you would ask me, and I would give you living water." John 4:10

Dear Lord,

You are the Peace I need. I have searched for what you freely give in so many empty places. Thank you for directing my path to your truths. I believe you have all I need and what I have been searching for. Thank you for this living water you provide so I don't have to ever thirst again.

In Jesus' name,

Amen

Today I am Grateful For: _____   _____

_____

Today I Get To: _____

_____

Candlelight Service

~

WE HAVE A TRADITION IN our family to attend a Candlelight service on Christmas Eve. We get dressed up and head to church in expectation of the joy we will be filled with there. After church, we enjoy a special holiday meal, we take turns sharing with one another what we are most grateful for, and then we exchange gifts. The tree is lit, Christmas music fills the house in anticipation of another Christmas filled with family memories to be tucked away for the ages.

I love the sounds of the old carols we sing at that church service. In an era where it's not necessary to be dressed up to attend church, it is nice to see so many in their Christmas outfits looking ready for an occasion befitting a KING!

"For unto us a Child is born, unto us a Son is given; And the government will be upon His shoulder. His name will be called Wonderful, Counselor, Mighty God, Everlasting Father, Prince of Peace." Isaiah 9:6

In attending the candlelight service, we are "Making Room" for His coming. We are preparing our hearts. At the service, we deliberately put away resentments and all the distractions from our hearts and minds and give priority to honoring this Christ child. To declare that He is our wonderful counselor. He is our Mighty God and our everlasting Father. He is the Prince of Peace. By rearranging our priorities to include this time of worship we are making room, preparing our minds through prayer, and reflection in the midst of all the busyness. We are literally preparing our hearts with thoughts and attitudes worthy to welcome a KING. We are making room for love, joy and peace.

Each day that you have taken up this devotional and chosen intentionally to sit and be with this Christ child you have been preparing Him room. You have allowed Him to enter in and rearrange your priorities so you can let go of offenses and take up forgiveness. You have reconciled relationships in this season of reconciliation. You are allowing God to create in you a clean heart, so you are ready when He comes. You know He is living within you and you are making room for Him to feel welcomed. You are taking the time needed to hear Him speak in those whispering tones directly to your heart. You have allowed Him to enter in and bring truth where Satan has tried to deceive you and steal the good gifts He has for you.

Transformation takes time, and you have been allowing the time needed for this in your life. This year you did not just transform your home with greenery and glimmer and baked goods. You have invited the God of lavish love and transforming grace to open your heart and mind to beauty within. It was there all along but so much had distracted you from seeing yourself as you truly are. You allowed God access your heart and mind and are now a personal testimony of the process of transformation.

We have taken this journey of transformation together. In spending daily time with Jesus our friend and Savior, we are serving as living reminders to those who know us. They are witnessing lives fully blessed and shaped by love. Rather than seeing us frantically working without pausing to catch our breath, they see us remembering to pause, give thanks, laugh and enjoy the season of Love.

Every step we've taken has been a process. We have invited God in and given Him the opportunity to show us a different way. He is teaching us to invite Him and His transforming presence into every moment. We are growing into a gift that is bringing beauty into our surroundings.

We know that not all our plans will work out but we are learning to not allow those unmet expectations to steal our joy. In effect, we are learning that in giving up our ideals we may get more than we ever dreamed of.

So, in lighting the candle at this years' Candlelight service, I will be reminded that God's light is shining through many of us brighter than in years gone by. And I for one am honored to be one of His light bearers!

"We now have this light shining in our hearts, but we ourselves are like fragile jars containing this great treasure. This makes it clear that our great power is from God, not of ourselves." 2 Corinthians 4:7

Dear Jesus,

Tonight, we celebrate you, the Christ child. You are King of Kings and Lord of Lords! You are our living hope. Thank you for the transformation you have done in my heart and mind. I celebrate your birth tonight. Continue to transform me into your likeness.

In Jesus' precious name,

Amen

Today I am Grateful For: _____ _____

_____

Today I Get To: _____

_____

_____

_____

_____

_____

_____

_____

_____

_____

_____

Christmas Day

THE GIFTS HAVE BEEN OPENED. The endless pieces of paper strewn across the floor, the bows and gift bags with tissue paper no longer fluffed in place. The Christmas tree is barren of any gifts lingering under the tree have been opened; but the laughter and joy remain fresh on our hearts. We have given and received the sweetest gift in a hug acknowledging: they loved their gift. If not in their hug, their face said it all perfectly.

I wonder, what are the gifts I have unwrapped this year from the Lord? What did I receive as I spend time with Him? As I allowed His spirit to fill me daily I saw this season through His eyes. There were new wonders and I am in awe of the fresh spirit I carried this Christmas season.

I enjoyed peace in place of exhaustion. I had opportunities to serve others without resentment and had the renewed joy of giving sacrificially. I sang new songs that he placed in my heart. I was able to encourage others who weren't remembering to use those 3 words, I Get To... to completely change their perspective. As I used them daily in my quiet time with the Lord, I was then reminded daily...I do not have to do this, rather I Get To!

I had a quiet confidence that came from daily returning to that solitary place with the Lord.

"For thus says the Lord God, The Holy One of Israel" "In return-ing and rest you shall be saved; In quietness and confidence shall be your strength." Isaiah 30:15

Together, we have allowed the Light of the World to enter ours. Because of Jesus birth, and our relationship with Him, the world and our piece of it included, has conquered the world. The dark hard season of Christmas was not so hard this year because we included the reason for the season in the center of our lives.

He has blessed us with gifts of: a little more patience, a lot more caring, a determination to let His light shine through us. The great-est gift: the bright reality of Christmas has made us more humble, grateful, compassionate.

I think about Mary and Joseph. When you have your first child you can't help but stare in disbelief. This tiny little one has been entrusted to you. To love and care for and you recount little toes and fingers. Yet I cannot help but wonder, as they knew this little one entrusted to them was the Son of God. The Messiah. He had come to save the world.

When they had heard the news, the angels had proclaimed they did not understand how it was all going to happen. But they, in faith walked on.

You picked up this book and began learning to Abide in Christ. You may, or may not have known what it would do for you or in you. But in faith, you read on.

"Teach me your way, O LORD, that I will live according to your truth; give me a pure heart, so that I may honor your name." Psalm 86:11

Abiding in Christ first of all means having a life-giving connec-tion to him. We are incomplete of who he created us to be when we live life apart from Him

This Christmas day, sit back and enjoy the gift of family being together. There are so many who would do anything in order to Get To... spend time with their family. Time is precious and not something to take for granted. Let the wrapping paper linger on the floor. Let the dishes gather around the sink as you gather to play games or put together those Legos. Read that story to your child. Cuddle up together at nap time. This is a magical day and it will never come again. Being present in the moments matters.

"Why, you do not even know what will happen tomorrow. What is your life? You are a mist that appears for a little while and then vanishes." James 4:14

Merry Christmas!

Dear Baby Jesus,

Happy Birthday! Oh, how we love you. On this day, I give you my heart freshly recommitted to you. And I thank you for every good gift you have given me during this Advent time as I prepared my heart for your birth. I love you Jesus and I want my life to show your love to a world that needs your love.

Thank you for blessing me with love of family and for making a way for me to spend eternity with you.

In Jesus' name,

Amen

Today I am Grateful For: _____ _____

_____

Today I Get To: _____

_____

_____

_____

_____

_____

_____

_____

_____

_____

_____

The Rush is Over

~᷉

IN TUCKING AWAY THE RIBBONS and bows let's be mindful to not tuck away our new-found faith and way of keeping our sanity among all the chaos of life.

Life gets messy, whether it is Christmas time or not. Our day to day lives are anything if not a maze of twist and turns. If it's not one thing trying to steal our joy its' another. As we begin to turn out attention on the coming year, let's keep our eyes focused on the One who helped us maneuver through the ins and outs of the last twenty-five plus days. While we would all agree we still have much to learn about walking in the Spirit each day, we can celebrate that we are on our way. We don't want to turn back to patterns that leave us exhausted, frustrated and empty.

"I am not saying that I have this all together, that I have it made. But I am well on my way reaching out for Christ, who has so wondrously reached out for me. Friends, don't get me wrong: By no means do I count myself an expert in all of this, but I've got my eye on the goal, where God is beckoning us onward – to Jesus. I'm off and running, and I'm not turning back. So, let's keep focused on that goal, those of us who want everything God has for us. If any of you have something else in mind, something less than total commitment, God will clear your blurred vision – you'll see it yet! Now that we're on the right track, let's stay on it." Philippians 3:12-16

God always honors His Word, regardless of whether our commitment is secure.

As He has begun this new work in our lives and people have seen the evidence of a life changed by spending time with Jesus it is important to be careful how we live. People are watching us. We can either enhance His reputation or choose to allow someone else to be His hands and feet. His voice. When we stay in a close relationship with the One who has the power to change us and everything about the way we live life – we will have whatever we need one day at a time.

How exciting for us to enter the New Year with this kind of solid confidence that comes from a life connected to the source of life. Whether you fully realize it or not, the growth you've had over this past few weeks is remarkable. When truth enters our lives, it changes everything. And to take it one step further, we can be the voice God uses to confirm His Word! Truth is truth regardless of whose lips carry it. If we are going to enter into the new year being His light and hope to a world looking for what we have then we must have eyes set on what God is doing.

We need to decide to be people of purity and power, character and living demonstrations of how life with Jesus can be completely different in such a better way than the world lives.

As we have walked the last days together one day at a time, having what we need as we need it. Jesus will be faithful to all He has promised.

"Because of the Lord's great love, we are not consumed; His compassions never fail. They are new every morning; great is your faithfulness." Lamentations 3:22-23

Long after all the decorations are down and this Christmas season is past, the Lord's faithfulness will still be alive, vibrant and available.

"The LORD delights in those who fear Him, who put their hope in His unfailing love." Psalm 147:11

We do not have to feel the pressure to perform for God. His ways are completely different than our ways and it really becomes a way of life to live out from the burden of a performance driven identity. What He is doing in us is something new. It's a special thing to know we start the new year with a new purpose. God is building on what is already been established.

"Salvation is not a reward for the good things we have done, so none of us can boast about it." Ephesians 2:9

"For I am about to do something new. See, I have already begun! Do you not see it? I will make a path through the wilderness. I will create rivers in dry wastelands." Isaiah 43:19

The struggles you had this past year are being smoothed out by God's sovereign hand. Sometimes we feel as if we have just been wandering around in circles, not seeing the progress we long for. The verse above is reassuring us-it is His power that will open up the path He has for you! I'll finish with this final promise in His Word!

"Being confident of this, that He who began a good work in you will carry it on to completion until the day of Jesus Christ." Philippians 1:6

Dear Lord,

I'm looking forward to this coming year. I will walk into it with my hand in yours. Thank you for all your promises to reassure me, I am not on this journey alone.

In Jesus' name,

Amen

Today I am Grateful For: _____   _____

Today I Get To: _____

_____

_____

_____

_____

_____

Seek My Face

⁓

DURING THE BUSY HOLIDAYS, I do fairly well with boundaries to protect what can already be an overfilled schedule. Once Christmas Day comes and goes can be a different story. I get a bit antsy wanting to get our home back to pre-Christmas décor and unclutter the house. I start letting my mind gaze into the days that are stretched before me. It's ok to make some plans but we should proceed with caution. Let's remember to hold those plans of ours tentatively, anticipating that God may have other ideas.

We are in a new season of walking in step with the Spirit. As this day and the ones to follow come, we are going to concentrate on the tasks before us while keeping our focus on the ONE who never leaves our side.

"The Lord himself goes before you and will be with you; He will never leave you nor forsake you. Do not be afraid; do not be discouraged." Deuteronomy 31:8

This assurance that we are walking side by side will help keep the clutter from our minds. We will be more open to the changes that naturally will come up in our day. As we choose to allow God to occupy more and more of our thoughts, we will become comfortable with the rhythm and pace He sets for us. As we surrender the need to control every moment of the day we will learn important lessons to follow. The path He prepared for us. The difficulties that might be part of your day can even be blessings when it draws us deeper into His presence.

Even though His presence is a guaranteed promise, that does not mean we may always feel like He is with us. We may have moments when we feel alone or just simply don't feel the peace that accompanies His presence. Negative emotions will look for ways to creep in. Here is the key. In those moments, you have a choice to ponder what you ponder.

"We demolish arguments and every pretension that sets itself up against the knowledge of God, and we take captive every thought to make it obedient to Christ." 2 Corinthians 10:5

If we are honest, much of our troubles comes from our own way of thinking. We get so set on what should or should not happen; we have an opinion about everything. We want what we want, when we want it. So, when something happens in our day or life or the lives of those we care about – it can really throw our worlds in a tailspin.

What the above scripture is trying to help us understand is this: We need to literally get rid of the voices in our head. Some may be voices of family members or one may be your own. We have to humble ourselves to admit, we are not wiser than God! We don't know what should happen in every given situation. We don't know what the best time frame is. We cannot see beyond today. Only God can and does! We either trust Him or we do not! The truth may be that you are learning to trust Him.

"To all perfection I see limit, but our commands are boundless." Psalm 119:96

We get so conditioned in this world that we want and expect perfection. But what is perfection? When everything works out according to "our" plans and time frame-is that perfection? Do we have an entitled mentality that puts defenses up whenever something or someone comes against our way of thinking? I am not sure when this way of thinking became normal, acceptable but it is not God's way.

As the verse above states, God's commands are boundless. He knows best! He does not have a book of rules to keep us from good, fun things; rather His commands are to help us know the difference between a good thing and a counterfeit blessing. There are many "good choices" you can make every day.

Think of it like this. There are three doors. Behind door number one is a bad choice, behind door number two is a good choice, and behind door number three is the best choice. All of these choices are things you can do today. You need to choose which tasks you will do. Keep in mind you do not know all your day holds. Now, let's say you know someone who knows exactly what is behind each door. And you have a relationship with them. They are willing to give you their input based on knowing you. Would you welcome their help or go it alone?

We have this same option every day. God is the only one who knows what our day holds. He is aware of your circumstances and is willing to guide you to the best decision. The choice is yours. You can spend time with Him and allow Him to direct your choices throughout the day- or go it alone.

We can get so conditioned to thinking "We have to do everything" but that is a trap. We Get To experience peace in the unexpected interruptions that come every day if we believe God is in control. It may still be hard to handle the curveballs thrown your way, but it will be much easier to know you are not handling them alone.

Dear Lord,

Thank you that your commands are set for my good. To protect me, not harm me. Help me grow in trusting you.

In Jesus' name,

Amen

Today I am Grateful For: _____ _____

_____

Today I Get To: _____

_____

The Voice of Encouragement

~⁀

"Therefore encourage one another and build each other up."

1 THESSALONIANS 5:11

AS THE YEAR COMES TO an end there are many people feeling let down. The past year holds so many hard losses unmet expectations. You may still be waiting for something you were sure would happen this year. You or someone you love needs to be encouraged to keep going. We are all either the one in need of or the one called to be the encouragement today.

Negative voices are contradictory to God's plan for our lives and only adds frustration to our circumstances and relationships. Daily we have a choice to focus on all that is disappointing and just plain wrong; or see how we can be the light of change in someone's life. Often, I have literally allowed someone to borrow my faith to get them to keep flaming the fire of their own faith.

Everyone needs encouragement! At the very heart of encouragement is a heart willing to listen. We may not agree with every aspect of someone's' life choices, but we can allow their differences to be a bridge. An opportunity to love on someone who just desperately needs to be heard. Differences can rip us apart or fill gaps and bring understanding and empathy for situations we may not have any knowledge about. So many times, we are just sent to encourage someone. It is not our job to change their thinking. After we have heard their deep needs and hurts we can bend our knees and pray for God to be working all things together for good for them.

We try to bring solutions when often, God is working on the solution while using us to be His love, opening a door for them to just make it to another day. Sometimes people are between a rock and a hard place. There are those who feel they have nothing to give, nothing to offer and we can direct them to One who doesn't need anything from them.

God meets each of us right where we are. Sometimes, God leads us through the desert, but other times it's a raging rivers. To get across, God provides stepping stones to move above the treacherous waters along His calm still waters.

"The Lord is my Shepard, I shall not want. He makes me lie down in green pastures; He leads me beside the still waters. He restores my soul; He leads me along paths of righteousness For His Names sake. Psalm 23:1-3

Righteousness is simply being in right standing with God. About seeking His plan and coming into agreement with His will for our lives on a daily basis.

Let's pray together that God's very real presence and power in our lives will draw others to Him. They'll see evidence of our close relationship with Him.

Don't try to hide the trials and struggles you have had in the past either. I believe God will (when you are ready) used your life story to encourage someone again and again. Your pain won't be in vain. It helps when others can look at our lives and see that while we are strong believers, we too have troubles and trials. Sometimes the trials have been ongoing for a long time. This testimony can speak directly to the one who has misunderstood that suffering is not from God.

Joseph was loved and chosen by God but suffered for years as a prisoner for crimes he did not commit. God allowed it for good.

"What Satan intended for evil God intended for good.

David was a man after God's own heart, yet he was forced to run and hide for his life. He was chosen as the anointed one to become King long before he became King. All the years of living homeless, having Saul trying to kill him were all suffering God allowed for good

Adversity is going to happen-we need to be reminded of truth. God is a good God. He knows the plans He has for us. They are good plans.

"For I know the plans I have for you." Declares the Lord, "plans to prosper you and not to harm you, plans to give you hope and a future." Jerimiah 29:11

We may not know what God's timing will be but this is a great promise to enter the new year and to encourage you or anyone that stands in need of hope.

"Those who wait for Me will not be put to shame." Isaiah 49:23

Dear Jesus,

You know all about my past year and have helped me have what I needed every day. You have lead me when I wasn't sure which way to go. Thank you for your promises. I am grateful that my future is in your hands. That what you have planned is good. I desire to allow your powerful presence to be evident in me every day and draw others to you.

In Jesus' name,

Amen

Today I am Grateful For: _____   _____

_____

Today I Get To: _____

_____

_____

_____

_____

Puzzle Pieces

THERE WERE TIMES IN MY childhood home where my mom would bring out the card table and empty out a 1000-piece puzzle for our family to work on. Sometimes it went quickly, but generally it would be a project that lasted several weeks. I recall watching my mom work on the puzzle; it seemed to relax her. As a young girl, I would begin trying to figure out the right place for the hundreds of random pieces and if I want able to get an area going I would soon head off in search of something else to do.

I wonder about our lives. We are very much like a puzzle. We add different experiences and people. We move here and there. Enjoy this hobby and that interest. We have thrilling fun and devastating losses. All these experiences add to the puzzle of our lives becoming a beautiful picture that God is designing. He is patient as His hands create the masterpiece He has already designed. He knows what He created. He knows what we will come out looking like. He knows just where the pieces need to be curved and cut in order to all fit into His perfect plan.

All too often we get discouraged and impatient when plans in our lives don't fit where or when we thought they would. When people seem to completely tear our lives apart. It can be hard to trust that even these pieces of our lives are really going to work out. It is a time of refinement as we chose to go by faith, not by sight. Or a time of rebellion, when in our fear, we run determining we can't trust God.

There have been multiple times in my life when during the difficulty I had no understanding of how God could be in the details. But every time, every time He was. While He did not cause the suffering, He was faithful right in the center it. When I tried to make sense of it, I never could. To this day I am not sure why some of these things were allowed, but this I know: Every difficult thing in my life has made me draw closer to God. While I was unsure of many things; I was never unsure of God being with me.

I know God sees me. I know He cares and I know if ever something could be used and not happen in vain, it would be by God's gracious hand. He always makes something beautiful rise up out of the ashes. This next scripture is Good news for the oppressed, bewildered and the brokenhearted.

"The Spirit of the Lord is upon me, for the Lord has anointed me to being good news to the poor. He sent me to comfort the broken hearted and to proclaim that the captives will be released and the prisoners set free. He has sent me to tell those who mourn that the time of the Lord's favor has come, and with it, the day of God's anger against his enemies. To all who mourn in Israel, he will give a crown of beauty for ashes, a joyous blessing instead of mourning, festive praise instead of despair. In their righteousness, they will be like great oaks that the Lord planted for His own glory." Isaiah 61:1-3

"God, pick up the pieces. Put me back together again. You are my praise!" Jerimiah 17:14

There was a child who loved putting puzzles together. His favorite one was 2 sided. On one side was a map of the world and on the other was a face of Jesus. The first time he put it together his parents were surprised at how quickly the young boy managed to piece the puzzle together since he did not have much knowledge of geography. When the boy's daddy asked him how he was able to do it he replied. "When the picture of Jesus was put together, the world looked right to me."

What truth there is in that. When we take our eyes off of all that is happening in our world and put our attention on the face of Jesus our world will look right to. What we choose to focus on will bring us into a better place with all the pieces that we are not yet familiar with.

As you enter this coming year, your heart may be struggling to want to go on. The pain that has ripped through our lives can have us questioning how we fit anymore.

Trust God! Like the children of Israel who had the enemy nipping at their heals, put your foot one foot in front of the other and watch God part the raging sea before you. God is drawn to the hurting and the broken. Allow His hand to take yours and allow His bright light to shine through you.

Every circumstance can be used for God's purpose, bound together by His loving plan. He who promised is faithful to complete what He has started.

Dear Lord,

Help me today trust in you Lord with all my heart. Help me to not lean on my own understanding. In every decision, help me acknowledge you as My Lord. Help me to believe that you are faith to complete what you have started and that with every piece of my life, you are making something beautiful and putting the pieces of my life back together again. Help me walk by faith, not by what I see. Surround me with your love. Thank you that I do not have to take one step without you right beside me.

In Jesus' name,

Amen

Today I am Grateful For: _____ _____

_____

Today I Get To: _____

_____

115

DECEMBER 30

Wonder

~

WITH THE CHILDREN, STILL OFF for the Christmas break, or some remaining family in town you may not know just what is on the docket for today. No matter what is going on in your corner of the world lets allow the wonder of the moments to bring us joy. To find contentment in the big and small details of our life.

Whether you are making breakfast, folding laundry, whipping up around the bathroom sink or making a bed, consider the wonder of it all. You Get To be making breakfast for those you love. You have the food, while others go without. You are folding clean laundry. You Get to take care of the loved ones and in the comfort of your home you wash and fold the tiniest of shirts and the new t-shirts you had stuck in your husbands stocking. Those water marks the were splashed around the sink as your sweet loved ones brushed teeth will one day be in a home of their own. You Get to hear the giggles and laughter that fills your home on a daily basis. And in making that bed that provided much needed rest, You Get to be warm and safe having a place to call home, a resting place.

All these little seemingly insignificant daily tasks are all reasons to praise God. There is Wonder in each moment. As you have learned to pause and sit before Jesus these December days, may you now take that discipline and apply it to all of your life. The moments in our day can fill us with wonder. What a gift to see the gift in each detail that He has planned and prepared for us.

If you are a caregiver, you know the work that goes into preparing the grocery list and the meals that come out of that effort. As you wash the clothes so the children can go into their closets and find everything they need to get dressed for their day. You are well aware of the effort that took. As you jump in the car to taxi this child to and from their activities, again, you made sure the car was safe and gassed up. We, as caregivers, do these things because we love our family and want to care for them.

"If you then, though you are of sinful nature know how to give good gifts to your children, how much more will your Father in Heaven give the Holy Spirit to those who ask Him?" Luke 11:13

The Holy Spirit guides us into all truth. His spirit leads us and regenerates us. The Holy spirit empowers us, fills us, teaches us. The Holy Spirit produces fruit in us and evidence of His work. The Spirit washes and renews us. The Holy Spirit is a gift given specifically to us, God's sons and daughters so we will know how to live this life that Jesus has planned for us.

The definition of Wonder (noun) A feeling of surprise mingled with admiration, caused by something beautiful, unexpected, unfamiliar or inexplicable.

(VERB) Think about, meditate on, reflect on, speculate about.

"For You are great and do wondrous deeds; You alone are God." Psalm 86:10

How many times have we driven to a familiar place and when we got there, we don't even really know how we got there. We did not take notice of the things around us as we drove, we made it through traffic lights but could not tell the color of cars at that same intersection. We can go in autopilot through much of our day.

To slow down and purposefully engage in Wonder is our assignment for today and the days to come. Wonder will cause our hearts to swell. We will feel the wind God gave to enable us to sail through the day. His beauty in the moments will be perceived out of intentionality. If we begin the discipline of seeking out the beauty He places before us we cannot exhaust it.

Wonder will remind us that nothing is random or wasted. Meaning is woven into everything. We can choose to walk through our days bored as we see everything as mundane and difficult OR we can look through eyes of grace. Knowing He is going before us.

Today, as you walk outside, take a deep breath of air. If it's cold, let it sting your lungs and fill your frame with and deep cleansing awakening. If it is warm, let the sun shine on your face and let it remind you that it is God who set the sun in place.

"Love the Lord God with all our passion and prayers and intelligence and energy." Mark 12:30

Wonder is a part of God's joyful strategy! Six little letters can bring a rich harvest, causing our lives to brim over at the vastness and mystery of life.

Dear Heavenly Father,

You bring wonderful moments into my life all day long. Thank you for all the things I Get To enjoy and have in my life. May you fill me with a new sense of wonder at even the day to day activities that make up my day. May I live a life of awareness at all the wonder you fill my life with.

In Jesus' name,

Amen

Today I am Grateful For: _____ _____

_____

Today I Get To: _____

_____

_____

_____

_____

_____

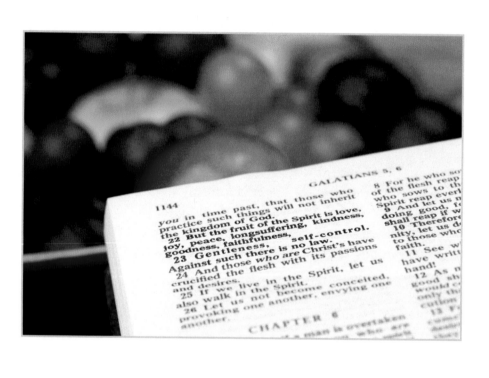

Whole

WITH THE NEW YEAR RIGHT around the corner many of us are making resolutions. Some of us have indulged a bit and our waistlines will need a little attention.

I was reading how Jesus mind was so pure and intentional on being whole. The best and truest version of who His Father had created Him to be. He was not easily diverted from the basic truths of His Father. He was nourished directly from His Father's hand. He did not look for imitations to being filled. He was fed by the purest, truest only source of wholeness directly from the Father's hand.

As we begin making resolutions, let's look to how Jesus was able to stay focused on His goal. He didn't need to diet. He wasn't drawn to comfort food. He did not put off until tomorrow what was the right thing for today. He knew His Father had the best and only necessary ingredients for sustaining His life and he never went looking for substitutions.

Considering how successful Jesus life was here on earth I for one want to begin this year as Jesus as my mentor to attaining wholeness in all areas of my life.

Our culture is all in a craze over identifying whole foods in their basic form. Organic is a word sought after as we weave in and out of the grocery aisles.

So, imagine sitting at a table with Jesus. what would he have prepared for us?

"You prepare a feast for me in the presence of my enemies. You honor me by anointing my head with oil. My cup overflows with blessings." Psalm 23:5

It is important to consider what enemies are at the table. I believe these are some of the enemies at the table, the ones that lure us to compromise, to frustration, to giving up or giving in. The enemy of "You're not good enough," the lies saying, "You have never succeeded before or you are too weak to finish this." The enemy of our past. The enemy of self-medicating through food, TV, shopping, working…. The enemy of exhaustion. The enemy of "you're all alone."

The lies of the enemy go on and on, but God is sitting at the table with us. He has spiritual foods for us. Food to sustain us and see us through all the false beliefs we have been ingesting.

"By His divine power, God has given us everything we need for living a Godly life. We have received all this by coming to know Him, the one who called us to himself by means of His marvelous glory and excellence. Because of His glory and Excellence, He has given us great and precious promises. These are the promises that enable you to share His divine nature and escape the world's corruption caused by human desires. In view of all this make every effort to respond to God's promises. Supplement your faith with a generous provision of moral excellence, and moral excellence with knowledge, and knowledge with self-control, and self-control with patient endurance, and patient endurance with Godliness, and Godliness with brotherly affection, and brotherly affection with love for everyone. The more you grow like this, the more productive and useful you will be in the knowledge of our Lord Jesus Christ." 2 Peter 1:3-8

The world wants us to believe that we can take bits and pieces of our relationship with God. Section Him off to only effect certain areas of our life. This is sadly the reality of many, but it's also a sad reality that those who live apart from God are not successful. The world continually lives void of contentment and out of balance. They cannot find a peace that satisfies. They continue tin search of the purpose of life. They do not know how to maintain joy in all circumstances. They do not know that the Joy of the Lord can be their strength.

Jesus craved the Whole truth of life with His Father. God's divine power gave Jesus everything He needed for life here on earth and it is available to us as well.

"His divine power has given us everything we need for life and Godliness through the full knowledge of the One who called us by His own glory and excellence: 2 Peter 1:3

Ask God to give you whole spiritual food. He has already prepared it for you; so feast on! Ask God what resolutions He has set for you this coming year. I, for one want to know I am in line to receive everything He has planned for me and I believe you do too.

Dear Heavenly Father,

I am in awe that you sit at a table with my enemies that you prepared just for me. It gives me such confidence to know you see me and are with me every day to help me. Thank you for providing all I need to live a life worthy of the call I have received. By your grace I desire to draw others to you. I love you and thank you for loving me.

In Jesus' name,

Amen

Today I am Grateful For: _____ _____

_____

Today I Get To: _____

_____

_____

_____

_____

_____

_____

_____

RUN YOUR RACE

As WE CONCLUDE OUR JOURNEY together you may be wondering what's next? I would say: "Run Your Race!"

Just as an athlete prepares for competition, we too have to prepare for winning in this life. What we have begun in December will be a great platform to continue training our hearts and minds to stay fit in our spiritual journey. The discipline of sacrificing a few minutes of sleep to spend time mentally preparing for the day ahead of us has served us well and will continue to do so into the new year.

So often, when the resolutions are still a thought in our heads, we wave January 1 out before us as the starting line. This year, we are ahead of the masses by beginning our training December 1. We did not wait. We did not make excuses. When we failed, we got right back on the journey to a closer walk with Jesus. He has been so proud of each of us as He has been training right alongside of us. God has a unique race mapped out specifically with us in mind. What He has in store is designed just for each one of us. He knows just what each of us needs and the way he has equipped us to run the race and He will continue to be faithful to train us one day at a time.

"I plead with you to give your bodies to God because of all He has done for you. Let them be a living and holy sacrifice-the kind He will find acceptable. This is truly the way to worship Him. Don't copy the behaviors and customs of this world, but let God transform you into a new person by

changing the way you think. Then you will learn what God's will is for you, which is good and pleasing and perfect.". Romans 12:1-2

We must keep in mind that our decisions will be contrary to much of the worlds' thinking. Our lives will be living testimonies to the power of putting Jesus and His ways first. The people in your circle of influence will see a wonderful transformation in you. God will use you and your peaceable spirit to draw people to Himself. This is part of the race He has chosen for us. We are all in a race of some sort whether we call it that or not.

"Do you not realize that in a race everyone runs, but only one person gets the prize? So, run to win. All athletes are disciplined in their training. They do it to win a prize that will fade but we do it for an eternal prize. So, we run with purpose in every step." 1 Corinthians 9:24-26a

Every day, we must decide to get into "spiritual shape" for the endurance of the day ahead of us. And it is key to remember we are not alone. Find someone who will help keep you accountable. Who understands the importance of the race you are training for.

"A person standing alone can be attacked and defeated, but two can stand back to back and conquer. Three are even better, for a triple braided cord is not easily broken." Ecclesiastes 4:12

You and another believer along with Jesus who is always by your side will enable you to stand stronger than if you try to train for this race alone. There will inevitably be life. Life's troubles will attempt to trip up our commitment to walking daily with Jesus.

"Therefore, since we are surrounded by such a huge crowd of witnesses to the life of faith, let us strip off every weight that slows us down, especially the sin that so easily trips us up. And let us run with endurance the race God has set before us. We do this by keeping our eyes on Jesus, the champion who initiates and perfects our faith. Because of the joy awaiting Him, He endured the cross, disregarding its shame. Now He is seated in the place of honor beside God's throne. Think of all the hostility he endured from sinful people, then you won't become weary and give up." Hebrews 12:1-4

Jesus knows first-hand what opposition is like. He knows what it may cost you to run this race, but He also knows what is at stake and the crown of glory that awaits you when you finish the race.

It certainly won't be easy. But the best things in life aren't. I want you to know I will be praying for you every day. I will be asking God to help you. To highlight His nearness and His power in each day. To send you encouragement just when you need it the most. I am asking God to speak His words of Life into you each day. That His word will become living and active each day.

"Press on towards the end of the race and receive the heavenly prize for which God, through Jesus Christ, is calling you." Philippians 3:14"

Dear Jesus,

Thank you for bringing each person into this season of Advent. Thank you for coming again into our daily lives, just as you promised you would. Father God, help each of us run the race you have uniquely mapped out for us. Help us allow you to equip us every day to go out and be your spiritual gangsters. We want to make your glory come alive through our living sacrificial lives.

I love you Lord.

In Jesus' name,

Amen

ABOUT THE AUTHOR

CINDY L. PENTECOST AND HER husband, Mark, are the owners of It Works!, the global sales company that has provided countless families with the opportunity to take control of their lifestyles and income. Cindy is the president of It Works! Gives Back, the charitable organization founded within the company that serves a variety of people, from victims of human trafficking and pediatric cancer to those devastated by natural disasters.

Cindy's mother raised her and her five sisters alone in Michigan, giving Cindy a valuable perspective on the importance of family. She and her husband have been married for forty years and were high school sweethearts. They have been blessed with three children; Kami, Kindsey, and Kyler (wife Kristi) and three grandchildren; Landon, Colton, and Skyler. Cindy has also adopted a family of four in Africa, and she considers them as much her family as those here at home.

Made in the USA
Columbia, SC
21 November 2021

49462167R00080